THE

EVERYTHING KIDS'

LEARNING SPANISH BOOK

Fun exercises to help you learn *español*

Laura K. Lawless

Adams Media

Avon, Massachusetts

Dedication

This book is dedicated to my beautiful new nephew Remi Justin.
I just know you're going to grow up and love language like I do!

EDITORIAL

Publisher: Gary M. Krebs
Director of Product Development: Paula Munier
Associate Managing Editor: Laura M. Daly
Associate Copy Chief: Brett Palana-Shanahan
Acquisitions Editor: Kate Burgo
Production Editor: Katie McDonough
Associate Production Editor: Casey Ebert

PRODUCTION

Director of Manufacturing: Susan Beale
Associate Director of Production: Michelle Roy Kelly
Cover Design: Erick DaCosta, Matt LeBlanc
Layout and Graphics: Heather Barrett,
Brewster Brownville, Colleen Cunningham,
Erin Dawson, Jennifer Oliveira

An Everything® Series Book.
Everything® and everything.com® are registered trademarks of F+W Publications, Inc.

Published by Adams Media, an F+W Publications Company
57 Littlefield Street, Avon, MA 02322. U.S.A.
www.adamsmedia.com

ISBN 10: 1-59337-716-9
ISBN 13: 978-1-59337-716-8
Printed in the United States of America.

J   I   H   G   F   E   D   C

This publication is designed to provide accurate and authoritative information with regard to the subject matter covered. It is sold with the understanding that the publisher is not engaged in rendering legal, accounting, or other professional advice. If legal advice or other expert assistance is required, the services of a competent professional person should be sought.

—From a *Declaration of Principles* jointly adopted by a Committee of the American Bar Association and a Committee of Publishers and Associations

Many of the designations used by manufacturers and sellers to distinguish their products are claimed as trademarks. When those designations appear in this book and Adams Media was aware of a trademark claim, the designations have been printed with initial capital letters.

Cover illustrations by Dana Regan.
Interior illustrations by Kurt Dolber.
Puzzles by Beth L. Blair.

This book is available at quantity discounts for bulk purchases.
For information, please call 1-800-289-0963.

See the entire Everything® series at *www.everything.com*.

CONTENTS

INTRODUCTION

Learning Spanish is fun, and you know why? Because it opens up whole new worlds to you. Spanish is one of the most commonly spoken languages in the world—hundreds of millions of people in dozens of countries speak it. You know Spanish is spoken in Spain, but did you know that it's also spoken in most of Central and South America, from Mexico to Chile? In fact, there are only a few countries in Latin America where Spanish isn't spoken, like Brazil and Belize. There are also millions of Spanish speakers in the United States and in other countries all over the world. So by learning Spanish, you'll be able to talk to all of these people and learn about the similarities and differences between their countries and cultures and your own.

Plus, if you can convince someone like your mom, dad, brother, sister, or best friend to learn Spanish with you, you'll be able to study and practice together. It's a lot more fun learning Spanish when you have someone to speak it with regularly. You can help each other understand the tricky parts and remember what you've learned. Then you'll also have a secret language that only the two of you understand!

Speaking Spanish is useful, too. If you want to travel to other countries, it makes sense to speak the local language. If you visit Argentina or Costa Rica, for example, it will be easier (and more fun!) to eat at restaurants, go shopping, and visit places like zoos and museums when you speak Spanish. Plus, when you go to high school, you have to study a foreign language. If you start learning Spanish now, you'll be ahead

ACKNOWLEDGMENTS

I would like to thank my best friend Lencho for helping me with my Spanish and making it fun at the same time. I'm also grateful to my many Spanish teachers who helped me fall in love with Spanish along the way. Some Spanish classes are dull, but I was very lucky most of the time. Last but definitely not least, I wish to thank the Spanish speakers I've met all over the world, particularly in Mexico, Costa Rica, and Spain (the only three Spanish-speaking countries I've been to so far). Your beautiful language is a perfect expression of your beautiful countries, and I appreciate your willingness to speak it with me—and your patience. ¡Muchísimas gracias!

of your classmates. Besides that, there are lots of jobs that need Spanish speakers. If you want to be a doctor, a teacher, or a lawyer when you grow up, knowing Spanish will let you talk to many more people than if you just know English. In fact, speaking Spanish will probably make it easier for you to get the job in the first place. And if find out that you like Spanish so much that you want to learn another language, like French or Italian, knowing Spanish will make learning that new language even easier.

The Everything KIDS' Learning Spanish Book will help you start learning Spanish and have fun at the same time. This is a complete introduction to Spanish written especially for kids just like you. Every chapter includes lessons, fun activities, puzzles, and games to help you learn, practice, and have a good time, too. You'll be able to talk about what you love and what you dislike, what you're studying at school, and what you want to do when you grow up. You'll also learn how to count, describe your family and friends, talk about clothes and food, and lots more. And when you've finished the whole book and are ready for more, there is a list of books and Web sites in the back to help you figure out where to go next. (There's also a glossary to help you remember how to say something in Spanish.)

Speaking Spanish is the first step to getting to know more about different countries, cultures, and people. It's fun to learn and speak, and it's useful too. So let's get started and have fun!

CHAPTER 1
The Basics
Los fundamentos

Alphabet—*Alfabeto*

The Spanish alphabet is similar to the English alphabet, except with one extra letter. Plus, the letters are pronounced differently in Spanish. Here is the Spanish alphabet, including how to say each letter, called pronunciation, spelled out for you.

Letter	Example	Pronunciation
A	for *abuelo* (grandfather)	AH
B	for *bueno* (good)	BEH
C	for *cama* (bed)	SEH
D	for *desayuno* (breakfast)	DEH
E	for *edificio* (building)	EH
F	for *falda* (skirt)	EF eh
G	for *gracias* (thank you)	HEH
H	for *hablar* (to talk)	AH cheh
I	for *Italia* (Italy)	EE
J	for *jamón* (ham)	HOH tah
K	for *kárate* (karate)	KAH
L	for *leer* (to read)	EL eh
M	for *madre* (mother)	EM eh
N	for *nieve* (snow)	EN eh
Ñ	for *ñame* (yam)	EN yeh
O	for *ocho* (eight)	OH
P	for *pelo* (hair)	PEH
Q	for *queso* (cheese)	KOO
R	for *regalo* (gift)	EHRR eh
S	for *sí* (yes)	ES eh
T	for *tener* (to have)	TEH
U	for *uno* (one)	OO
V	for *ventana* (window)	BEH
W	for *watt* (watt)	DO bleh beh
X	for *xerocopia* (photocopy)	EH kees
Y	for *ya* (already)	ee gree EH gah
Z	for *zapato* (shoe)	SEH tah

Alphabet Code

This puzzle looks like it is in code, but you are actually practicing how to sound out the Spanish *alfabeto* (alphabet)! Write the correct letter under each letter sound to find the answer to this riddle:

What kind of insect does well in school?

AH

____

ESeh   PEH   EH   ELeh   ELeh   EE   ENeh   HEH

____ ____ ____ ____ ____ ____ ____ ____

BEH   EH   EH

____ ____ ____

A = AH   L = ELeh

B = BEH   N = ENeh

E = ESeh   P = PEH

G = HEH   O = OH

I = EE   S = ESeh

UNO. OO, ENeh, OH UNO.

¡Bueno!

First sing the alphabet song in English. Easy, right? Now, try singing the alphabet song in Spanish! The new pronunciations and the extra letter might make it tricky, but don't give up. Keep practicing until you can sing the whole song without making a mistake!

Numbers—*Números*

Learning how to count in Spanish is lots of fun and very useful. Once you learn the numbers in Spanish, you can count all kinds of things, like pieces of fruit in the refrigerator, clothes in your closet, or birds in a tree in your backyard. Check out the numbers in the following list:

Number	In Spanish	Pronunciation
0	*cero*	SEH ro
1	*uno*	OO noh
2	*dos*	DOS
3	*tres*	TREHS
4	*cuatro*	KWA tro
5	*cinco*	SEEN ko
6	*seis*	SEHEES
7	*siete*	SEE EH teh
8	*ocho*	O cho
9	*nueve*	NUEH beh
10	*diez*	dee EHS
11	*once*	ON seh
12	*doce*	DO seh
13	*trece*	TREH seh
14	*catorce*	ka TOR seh
15	*quince*	KEEN seh
16	*dieciséis*	dee eh see SEHEES
17	*diecisiete*	dee eh see SEE EH teh

¡CUIDADO!
Mistake to Avoid

Though they're different in English, the letters B and V are pronounced exactly the same way in Spanish. The letters are both pronounced "beh," and they make a sound much like the B in English. There is no English V sound in Spanish.

Number	In Spanish	Pronunciation
18	*dieciocho*	dee eh see OH choh
19	*diecinueve*	dee eh see NUEH beh
20	*veinte*	BAIN teh
21	*veintiuno*	bain tee OO noh
22	*veintidós*	bain tee DOHS
23	*veintitrés*	bain tee TRES
24	*veinticuatro*	bain tee KWA troh
25	*veinticinco*	bain tee SEEN koh
26	*veintiséis*	bain tee SEHEES
27	*veintisiete*	bain tee SEE EH teh
28	*veintiocho*	bain tee OH choh
29	*veintinueve*	bain tee NUEH beh
30	*treinta*	TRAIN tah
31	*treinta y uno*	TRAIN tah ee OO noh
32	*treinta y dos*	TRAIN tah ee DOS
. . .		
40	*cuarenta*	kwa REN tah
41	*cuarenta y uno*	kwa REN tah ee OO noh
42	*cuarenta y dos*	kwa REN tah ee DOHS
. . .		
50	*cincuenta*	seen KWEN ta
60	*sesenta*	seh SEN tah
70	*setenta*	seh TEN tah
80	*ochenta*	oh CHEN tah
90	*noventa*	noh VEN tah
100	*cien*	SEE EN
1,000	*mil*	MEEL
1,000,000	*millón*	mee YON

Jumping Numbers

A frog wants to cross the pond, but he can only jump on lily pads with even numbers. Can you help him find the correct path from *el principio* (the start) to *el fin* (the end)? Hint: The frog can jump straight ahead, left, or right, but not diagonally.

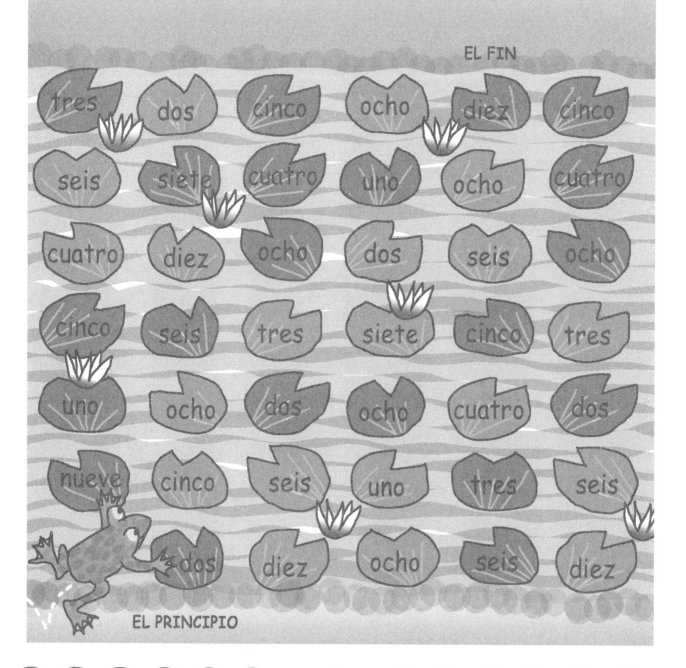

EL FIN

tres	dos	cinco	ocho	diez	cinco
seis	siete	cuatro	uno	ocho	cuatro
cuatro	diez	ocho	dos	seis	ocho
cinco	seis	tres	siete	cinco	tres
uno	ocho	dos	ocho	cuatro	dos
nueve	cinco	seis	uno	tres	seis
dos	diez	ocho	seis	diez

EL PRINCIPIO

To practice using the Spanish numbers, go around your house and count how many of the following items you see. Write your answers in the blank spaces. So, for example, if there are five clocks in your house, your response would look like this:

clocks   *cinco*

beds   _____

rugs   _____

sinks   _____

televisions   _____

telephones   _____

computers   _____

Gramática — Additional Grammar

When talking about twenties, thirties, etc., the Spanish numbers are the "tens" word (*veinte*, *treinta*, etc.) plus the "ones" word (*uno*, *dos*, etc.) joined by *y* (and). In the twenties, these three words join together in a single word and *y* becomes *i*. For the thirties and up, the three words stay separate. See the list of numbers for more examples.

Essential Vocabulary—*Vocabulario esencial*

When you're learning a new language, you often need to ask a lot of questions. This is when your essential vocabulary comes into play. This includes all the question and answer words you know in English. Check out the following list, and try pronouncing these essential Spanish words.

English	Spanish	Pronunciation
yes	*sí*	SEE
no	*no*	NOH
I don't know	*no sé*	no SEH
OK	*de acuerdo*	deh ah KWER doh
who	*quién*	KEE EN

Consejo
IMPORTANT TIP

When you ask a question in Spanish, you need a regular question mark at the end of the question, as well as an upside-down question mark at the beginning. For example, the question "What?" is written ¿Cómo? And for exclamations, there's an upside-down exclamation point to use at the beginning, like this: ¡Ay, caramba! (My goodness!) Grab a piece of paper and practice writing these new punctuation marks.

English	Spanish	Pronunciation
what	qué	KEH
when	cuándo	KWAN doh
where	dónde	DON deh
why	por qué	por KEH
how	cómo	KOH moh
and	y	ee
or	o	o

Now try practicing some of these essential Spanish words by answering the following questions. These are "yes or no" questions, so you can answer with either sí or no. Write your answers in the blank spaces.

Does your family have a pet? _____

Do you like the color blue? _____

Do you like to read books? _____

Have you ever been to the zoo? _____

Do you enjoy playing sports? _____

Now that you know these essential words, try putting them into sentences. The following are very useful sentences to use when you need to ask questions or get more information.

English	Spanish	Pronunciation
I have a question.	Tengo una pregunta.	TEN goh OO nah preh GOON tah
What does ___ mean?	¿Qué quiere decir ___?	keh KEE EH reh deh SEER
How do you say ___ in Spanish?	¿Cómo se dice ___ en español?	KOH moh seh DEE seh ___ en es PAH neeol

If you need someone to repeat something or speak more slowly, you can try these useful phrases:

English	Spanish
What?	*¿Cómo?*
I am sorry, I don't understand.	*Perdón, no comprendo.*
Repeat, please.	*Puede repetir, por favor.*
Please, more slowly.	*Más despacio, por favor.*
One more time, please.	*Otra vez, por favor.*

Nouns—*Nombres*

A noun is a person, place, thing, or idea. For example, here are some nouns in English:

- **Person:** mother, astronaut, Tommy, Mr. Smith
- **Place:** home, space, Chicago, Ireland
- **Thing:** book, suit, city, country
- **Idea:** love, happiness, anger, faith

In Spanish, nouns have what is called "gender," which means that every noun is either masculine or feminine. When you are talking about people and animals, gender makes sense; some people and animals are masculine (boys, men, lions) and some are feminine (girls, women, lionesses). But for other words, gender can seem funny. For example, cheese is masculine (*el queso*) and milk is feminine (*la leche*). But the gender for these nouns is not meant to say cheese is like a boy and milk is like a girl; the gender is just part of the name of each word.

Now, here are some common nouns and their translations in Spanish. Pay attention to the words *el* and *la* that come before each Spanish noun.

Gramática —
Additional Grammar

You can tell if a word is masculine or feminine by the word that comes in front of it: *un* and *el* are used for masculine nouns, and *una* and *la* are used for feminine nouns. Also, most Spanish nouns that end in *o* are masculine, and most nouns that end in *a* are feminine. Just be careful, because this isn't always the case!

la chica

English	Spanish	English	Spanish
the father	*el padre*	the mother	*la madre*
the boy	*el chico*	the girl	*la chica*
the cheese	*el queso*	the milk	*la leche*
the love	*el amor*	the happiness	*la felicidad*

El and *la* are called "definite articles" and are used when you want to talk about a specific noun. For example, "The book is on the table." You are talking about a specific book and a specific table, so you use the definite articles: *El libro está sobre la mesa*.

Un and *una* are called "indefinite articles" and are used when you are not talking about a specific noun. For example, "Do you have a hat and a scarf?" You are asking whether the person has one of these, so you use the indefinite articles: *¿Tienes un sombrero y una bufanda?*

Besides gender, Spanish nouns also have "number." This is easier because it's just like in English: nouns are either singular (just one) or plural (more than one). Spanish has special definite articles and indefinite articles for plural nouns. For example:

English (singular)	Spanish (singular)
the father	*el padre*
a father	*un padre*
the mother	*la madre*
a mother	*una madre*

English (plural)	Spanish (plural)
the fathers	*los padres*
some fathers	*unos padres*
the mothers	*las madres*
some mothers	*unas madres*

Verbs—*Verbos*

A verb is an action word: It says what is happening or how something is. Here are some verbs you already know in English:

- to do
- to go
- to want
- to listen to
- to be
- to play
- to hope

Verbs have many different forms, called "conjugations." Verbs change depending on whether the action is in the present, past, or future, and they also change depending on who is doing the action or being a certain way. For example:

I am going to the store.
You eat a lot.
He walks every day.

The words *I, you, he, she, we,* and *they* are called "subject pronouns." Here are Spanish subject pronouns with their pronunciations:

> ## ¡CUIDADO!
> ### Mistake to Avoid
>
> There are four words for "you" in Spanish. There are different words for "you" when talking to a friend or to an adult: *tú* is used when you talk to a friend and *usted* (often abbreviated *Ud.*) is used when you talk to an adult. Then there are also plurals that are used in different countries. For example, you use *vosotros* when you are talking to more than one friend in Spain, and *ustedes* (abbreviated *Uds.*) when you are talking to more than one adult in Spain, or to a group of people, friends and adults alike, in Spanish-speaking countries besides Spain.

English	Spanish	Pronunciation
I	yo	YOH
you	tú	TOO
you all	ustedes/vosotros	ooS TEH dehs/boh SOH tros
you (formal)	usted	oo STED
you (formal, plural)	ustedes	oo STED es
he	él	EHL
she	ella	EH ya
we	nosotros	noh SOH tros
they (masculine, mixed gender)	ellos	EH eeos
they (feminine)	ellas	EH eeas

Hey You!

One kid is talking to an adult teacher, while the other is talking to a cousin the same age. Start at the dot under each word. Follow the maze to find out who is talking to whom!

Conjugations are very important. In Spanish, the conjugation is different for every person doing the action, which means that you can actually leave out the subject pronoun, because the verb tells you who is doing the action. For example:

English	Spanish	Spanish (without subject pronoun)
I am going to the store.	*Yo voy al mercado.*	*Voy al mercado.*
You are going to the store.	*Tú vas al mercado.*	*Vas al mercado.*
He is going to the store.	*Él va al mercado.*	*Va al mercado.*

Each time you learn a new verb, you have to learn how it is conjugated. But this is not as difficult as it sounds because

many verbs follow the same patterns for conjugation. All verbs end in *-ar, -er,* or *-ir,* and this ending determines how they will be conjugated. For example, *hablar* (to speak) is an *-ar* verb.

English	Spanish
I speak	*yo hablo*
you speak	*tú hablas*
he speaks	*él habla*

Some other common *-ar* verbs are *amar* (to love), *ayudar* (to help), *lavar* (to wash), and *pagar* (to pay).

Comer (to eat) is an *-er* verb.

English	Spanish
I eat	*yo como*
you eat	*tú comes*
he eats	*él come*

Here are a few more *-er* verbs: *aprender* (to learn), *beber* (to drink), *deber* (to have to), and *leer* (to read).

Abrir (to open) is an *-ir* verb, and *-ir* verbs are conjugated just like *-er* verbs.

English	Spanish
I open	*yo abro*
you open	*tú abres*
he opens	*él abre*

Some useful *-ir* verbs are: *asistir* (to attend), *describir* (to describe), *escribir* (to write), *vivir* (to live).

Some verbs are irregular, which means that they don't follow these conjugation patterns. You'll learn how to conjugate the most common irregular verbs later in this book.

Gramática —
Additional Grammar

To say "it" in Spanish, you have to know the gender of the word you are replacing. If the word is masculine, use *él* and if it's feminine, use *ella.* For example, in the sentence "The book is red," you can replace "the book" with "it": "It is red." In Spanish, The book is red is translated as *El libro es rojo.* To say "It is red," you say, *Él es rojo.* Here's another example. In English: "The table is pretty; it is pretty." In Spanish: *La mesa es bonita; ella es bonita.*

Pronunciation and Spelling— *Pronunciación y ortografía*

Pronunciation means the way that you say a word. Spanish pronunciation is very easy. In fact, it's easier than English pronunciation, because Spanish does not have lots of silent letters and all kinds of different sounds for each vowel. Spanish has one sound for each vowel:

Vowel	Pronunciation
A	"ah" like in "father"
E	"eh" like in "bed"
I	"ee" like in "meek"
O	"oh" like in "go"
U	"oo" like in "moon"

Most of the consonants are very easy too:

Consonant	Pronunciation
B and V	like the b in "boy"
D	like the d in "do"
F	like the f in "father"
K and Q	like the k in "kite"
L	like the l in "live"
M	like the m in "mother"
N	like the n in "no"
P	like the p in "put"
S and Z	like the s in "see"
T	like the t in "take"
W (rare in Spanish)	like the w in "water"
Y	like the y in "yes"

The rest of the Spanish letters are different than the English ones, but with a little practice they are very easy too.

¿Cómo?— Say What?

Spanish has two other sounds you need to know. First, *ll* is called "EL yay" and is pronounced like the y in "yes." Some words that include *ll* are *llamar* (to call), *la calle* (street), and *ella* (she). And *ch* is pronounced like the ch in "cheese." This is found in words like *un cheque* (check), *mucho* (a lot), and *un muchacho* (boy).

Letter	Pronunciation
H	always silent
Ñ	like the ni in "onion"
J	sound does not exist in English, but the closest sound is like the h in "hello"
R	sound does not exist in English; this is called a "rolled r" because it's pronounced by letting your tongue roll against your teeth.
C and G	When C is followed by A, O, U, or a consonant, it is pronounced like the *c* in "cat." When C is followed by E or I, it is pronounced like the *c* in "cell." When G is followed by A, O, U, or a consonant, it is pronounced like the *g* in "give." When G is followed by E or I, it is pronounced like the Spanish J.
X	Sometimes it is pronounced like the x in "tax." Other times, it is pronounced like the x in "exist."

Pronunciation and spelling are much more closely related in Spanish than in English. The only Spanish letters that cause any real problems with spelling are H (because it's silent) and B and V (because they sound the same). Other than those, what you hear is what you write. Compared to English, with silent letters at the beginning of words (like the K in "knife"), in the middle of words (like the G in "sign"), and at the end of words (like the B in "lamb"), Spanish pronunciation is a piece of cake!

Consejo
IMPORTANT TIP

The stress in a Spanish word is indicated by an accent mark. The accent means that you should put extra emphasis on that syllable. For example, the Spanish word for pencil is *lápiz*, which is pronounced LA pees. If there is no accent, word stress falls on the last letter of the word. If the word ends in a vowel, N, or S, the stress is on the second to last syllable: *madre* — MA dreh. If the word ends in anything else, stress is on the last syllable: *calor* — ka LOR.

Now that you've learned a little bit about pronunciation, it's time to try speaking some Spanish aloud! Grab a parent or friend and ask if he or she would like to practice with you. Then take turns saying each of the following words aloud. Use the hints if you forget how to pronounce a letter.

Spanish	English	Pronunciation Hint
pollo	chicken	*ll* sounds like the English "y"
verde	green	*v* sounds like "b"
sueño	dream	*ñ* sounds like "ni" in "onion"
queso	cheese	*qu* sounds like the "k" in "kite"
joya	jewel	*j* sounds like the English "h"
hora	hour	*h* is silent

Now that you've had practice saying these words aloud, try having a little conversation with your parent or friend. You can use some of these same words to create a silly conversation using both English and Spanish. Here's an example:

Jane: Hi, Billy.
Billy: Hello.
Jane: Do you like ____pollo?____
Billy: Yes! I especially like it with ___queso.___
Jane: Me too. What's your favorite color?
Billy: I really like ___verde.___
Jane: Wow! That's the color of the ___joya___ in my necklace.

Now use some of these words to write your own silly Spanish-and-English conversation:

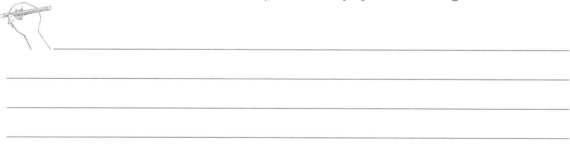

CHAPTER 2

Being Polite
Tener buenos modales

**¿Cómo?—
Say What?**

Expressions like *¿Cómo estás?* and *¿Qué tal?* are good to use when you're talking to a friend. But if you're talking to an adult, you would need to use the formal version: *¿Cómo está usted?* If you are talking to more than one adult, you would say, *¿Cómo están ustedes?*

Hi, how are you?—*Hola, ¿cómo estás?*

What's the first thing you say when you greet a friend? Probably, "Hello," right? In English, there are lots of ways to greet people. For example, you can say "Hi," "Hey," or "What's up?" Just like English, Spanish has several different ways to greet people. Here are some common greetings:

English	Spanish
Hi, Hello	*Hola*
Good morning, Good day	*Buenos días*
Good afternoon	*Buenas tardes*
Good evening	*Buenas noches*

The Spanish language has all kinds of different ways to ask "how are you?" too.

English	Spanish
How are you?	*¿Cómo estás?*
How's it going?	*¿Qué tal?*
What's new?	*¿Qué hay de nuevo?*
	¿Qué hay de bueno?
	¿Qué cuentas?
	¿Qué es de tu vida?

If someone asks you how you are doing, you can answer with one of the following responses:

English	Spanish
I'm good	*(Estoy) bien*
I'm great	*(Estoy) muy bien*
Nothing (is new)	*Nada*
No news	*Sin novedad*
Nothing much	*Nada de particular*

Buenas noches.

Night and Day

First collect all the dark letters and put them next to the sleepy *niña* (girl). Then collect all the white letters and put them next to the wide-awake *niña*. Use the letters to spell two common Spanish greetings as suggested by the pictures! Write the greetings on the lines provided.

Hint: Don't forget to include the accent on one of the letters!

English	Spanish
And you?	¿Y tú?
Same here	Igualmente
Me too	Yo también

Now that you know some basic greetings and responses, why not try a short dialogue? Sit down with a parent or friend and make up a short Spanish conversation. Here's a sample:

EVA: *Hola.*
JORGE: *Buenas tardes.*

EVA: *¿Qué tal?*
JORGE: *Bien. ¿Y tú?*

EVA: *Muy bien, gracias.*

Now fill in the blank spaces with some of the phrases you've learned and create your own dialogue. When you're finished, practice saying it out loud with your parent or friend.

SPEAKER 1: _____

SPEAKER 2: _____

SPEAKER 1: _____

SPEAKER 2: _____

Consejo
IMPORTANT TIP

As mentioned in Chapter 1, using subject pronouns is usually optional. So, if someone asks you *¿Cómo estás?* (How are you?), you can either respond with *Estoy bien* (I am well) or just *Bien* (well).

My name is...—*Me llamo...*

When you meet new people, one of the first things you always do is tell each other your names. Here are some common ways to introduce yourself or someone else and learn other people's names in English and Spanish:

English	Spanish
What's your name?	*¿Cómo te llamas?* (informal)
	¿Cómo se llama? (formal)
Who are you?	*¿Quién eres?*
My name is…	*Me llamo…*
This is…	*Éste es…*
His name is…	*Él se llama…*
Her name is…	*Ella se llama…*
It's nice to meet you.	*Mucho gusto.*

Now fill in the following sentence with your own name:

Me llamo _____

Names are different in all different parts of the world. Living in the United States, you might have some friends with names like Michael or Benjamin and Jennifer or Amy. In Spanish speaking countries, however, people have very different names. Here are some common boys' and girls' names you might encounter in a Spanish speaking country:

Choose a Spanish name to use when you're practicing speaking Spanish. It doesn't have to be one similar to your real name; in fact, sometimes it's more fun to have a name that's completely different! For example, if your real name is Lindsay, you might like to go by Rosa in your Spanish class or when you're practicing Spanish at home.

Boys' Names

Alejandro	Enrique	José	Nacho
Antonio	Jaime	Juan	Pablo
Arturo	Javier	Julio	Paco
Carlos	Jesús	Luis	Pedro
Diego	Jorge	Miguel	Pepe

Girls' Names

Amalia	Cristina	Jessica	Nuria
Ana	Elena	Juanita	Pilar
Blanca	Eva	Lupe	Rosa
Camila	Francisca	María	Sara
Catalina	Isabel	Nadia	Violeta

Me llamo Rosa.

Hi, Llama!

This *niño* (boy) wants to say a proper "Hi!" to this friendly llama. How does he do it?

Fill in all the boxes with a dot in *el centro* (the center) to find out!

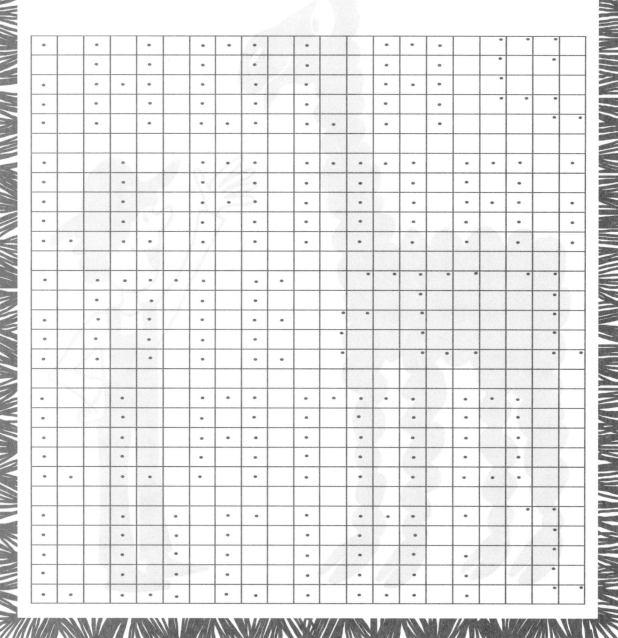

When you are talking to adults, you probably don't call them by their first names, right? Instead, you use a title plus their last name. For example, you might call your teacher Mr. Smith. Well, it's the same thing in Spanish:

English	Spanish	Spanish abbreviation
Mr.	*Señor*	*Sr.*
Mrs.	*Señora*	*Sra.*
Miss	*Señorita*	*Srta.*
Dr.	*Doctor*	*Dr.*
	Doctora	*Dra.*
Teacher	*Profesor*	*Prof.*
	Profesora	*Profa.*

So, if your neighbor is named Mr. Grant, you would call him Señor Grant. If your Spanish teacher is named Mrs. Juárez, you would call her Profesora Juárez. It's that easy!

Gramática — Additional Grammar

If you were talking about a person, instead of to him or her, you would need to use the definite article (*el* or *la*) and not capitalize the title: *La señora Vázquez no está aquí* (Mrs. Vázquez isn't here), *El doctor Ortega vive en Madrid* (Dr. Ortega lives in Madrid).

Questions—*Preguntas*

Just like in English, you can ask "yes or no" questions in Spanish by raising your voice at the end of any sentence. Try it with the following questions:

English	Spanish
Is Miguel ready?	*¿Está listo Miguel?*
Are you thirsty?	*¿Tienes sed?*

Questions that don't have a yes or no answer are a little different. They ask for information, like who, what, when, where, why, and how:

Consejo — IMPORTANT TIP

When you ask a question and you're pretty sure that the answer will be yes, you might add "right?" to the end of the sentence. You can also do this in Spanish by putting *¿no?* or *¿verdad?* at the end of the sentence. For example: Miguel is ready, right? *Miguel está listo, ¿verdad?* You're thirsty, right? *Tienes sed, ¿no?*

¡CUIDADO!
Mistake to Avoid

If someone speaks to you and you don't hear him the first time, you may say, "What?" to ask him to repeat himself. In Spanish, you can use *¿qué?* when you are asking a question with "what," like *¿Qué haces?* But when you just want to say "what?" because you didn't hear what someone said, it's more polite to say *¿cómo?*

English	Spanish
who	*quién*
what	*qué*
when	*cuándo*
where	*dónde*
why	*por qué*
how	*cómo*
how much	*cuánto*

To ask "who?" feels or is a certain way, just use *quién* plus a verb:

English	Spanish
Who is ready?	*¿Quién está listo?*
Who is thirsty?	*¿Quién tiene sed?*

Questions, Questions
Follow the lines over and under to learn who is who, and what is what!

quién · dónde · cuándo · qué · what · where · who · when

To ask questions with the other words, use the question word plus the verb. If you want to include the subject pronoun (such as *tú*), put it after the verb:

English	Spanish
What are you doing?	*¿Qué haces? ¿Qué haces tú?*
When are we eating?	*¿Cuándo comemos? ¿Cuándo comemos nosotros?*
Where is Ana?	*¿Dónde está Ana?*

Please and Thank You—*Por favor y gracias*

As you know, it's always important to be polite. It's just the same when you're speaking Spanish, so don't forget the magic words "please" and "thank you."

English	Spanish
please	*por favor*
pretty please	*porfis, por favorcito*
May I ... ?	*¿Puedo ... ?*
I want	*Quiero, Deseo*
I would like	*Quisiera*
thank you	*gracias*
thank you very much	*muchas gracias*
Thank you so much!	*¡Cuánto te lo agradezco!*
I thank you	*Le doy gracias*
you're welcome	*de nada*
don't mention it	*no hay de qué*

If you accidentally bump into someone or do something wrong, the polite thing to do is say you're sorry, right? It's the same in Spanish. The following are some words to use when you need to excuse yourself or apologize:

¿Cómo?— Say What?

When someone sneezes, the Spanish way to say "bless you!" is *¡Salud!* or *¡Jesús!* If a person sneezes more than once, Spanish speakers will sometimes say something after each sneeze. For example: for 1 sneeze it's *salud* (health); for 2 sneezes it's *dinero* (money) or *salud y dinero*; for 3 sneezes it's *amor* (love) or *salud y dinero y amor*; for 4 sneezes it's *alergias* (allergies). Try this out the next time someone in your family sneezes!

¡Muchas gracias!

¡CUIDADO!
Mistake to Avoid

Perdón, dispense, and *con permiso* are used to be polite, like when you interrupt someone or need someone to move over so that you can get by. *Perdóname* and *discúlpame* are used when you have done something wrong and are asking for forgiveness, like if you broke something or made a mess.

English	Spanish
pardon me	*perdón, dispense*
excuse me	*con permiso*
forgive me	*perdóname, discúlpame*
I'm sorry	*lo siento*
I'm very sorry	*lo siento mucho*

Goodbye—*Adiós*

Just like there are several ways to greet people in Spanish, there are also various ways to say goodbye. Here are some common phrases to use when you part ways:

English	Spanish
Goodbye	*Adiós*
Bye	*Chao*
Bye-bye	*Adiosito*
See you later	*Hasta luego*
	Hasta pronto
	Hasta la vista
Catch you later!	*¡Nos vemos!*
See you tomorrow	*Hasta mañana*
See you next week	*Hasta la semana próxima*
Have a nice day	*Que tengas un buen día*
	Que pases un buen día
Good night	*Buenas noches*

There are also some expressions that are only used for special kinds of goodbyes.

When someone is leaving on a trip, you can say *¡Buen viaje!* (Have a good trip!)

If your friend is taking a test, competing, or doing something else difficult, you can say ¡*Buena suerte!* (good luck!) or ¡*Que te vaya bien!* (I hope it goes well!)

When saying goodbye to someone they don't expect to see again for a long time, some Spanish speakers might say *Vaya con Dios* (Go with God).

Conversations—*Conversaciones*

Now that you know all this new vocabulary, it's time to practice with a friend! Here is a sample conversation to help you get started:

Speaker	English	Spanish
JAIME	Hello.	*Hola.*
LUPE	Hello. What's your name?	*Hola. ¿Cómo te llamas?*
JAIME	My name is Jaime, and you?	*Me llamo Jaime, ¿y tú?*
LUPE	My name is Lupe.	*Me llamo Lupe.*
JAIME	It's nice to meet you.	*Mucho gusto.*
LUPE	Same here.	*Igualmente.*
JAIME	How are you?	*¿Cómo estás?*
LUPE	Fine, and you?	*Bien, ¿y tú?*
JAIME	Same here.	*Igualmente.*
LUPE	Goodbye, Jaime.	*Adiós, Jaime.*
JAIME	Goodbye.	*Adiós.*

Here's another conversation. This one is between a boy named Miguel and his teacher, Mrs. López:

Gramática —
Additional Grammar

¡*Que te vaya bien!* is what you would say to a friend. But if you are saying "good luck" to an adult, you would need to say ¡*Que le vaya bien!* And if you are wishing good luck to more than one person, you have to say ¡*Que les vaya bien!*

Consejo
IMPORTANT TIP

Did you notice the upside-down question marks in the conversation between *Jaime* and *Lupe*? They have to be in front of the question, not at the beginning of the line. For example, in the sentence *Nada, ¿y tú?*, "*nada*" is the answer to a question, and then the question "*y tú*" comes after it. So the upside-down question mark goes in front of *y*.

Diversión—Fun Stuff

Now that you've read the sample conversations, make up your own! Use Spanish names and as much vocabulary as you can. For example, try one where your friend is leaving on a trip to Spain, and another where your brother or sister is taking a driving test.

Speaker	English	Spanish
MIGUEL	Good afternoon, Mrs. López.	*Buenas tardes, Señora López.*
SRA. LÓPEZ	Good afternoon, Miguel.	*Buenas tardes, Miguel.*
MIGUEL	How are you?	*¿Cómo está Ud.?*
SRA. LÓPEZ	Very good. Who is this?	*Muy bien. ¿Quién es ella?*
MIGUEL	Pardon me, Mrs. López, this is my sister. Her name is Blanca.	*Perdón, Señora López, es mi hermana. Ella se llama Blanca.*
SRA. LÓPEZ	It's nice to meet you.	*Mucho gusto.*
BLANCA	Good afternoon, Mrs. López.	*Buenas tardes, Señora López.*
SRA. LÓPEZ	Goodbye, Miguel and Blanca.	*Adiós, Miguel y Blanca.*
MIGUEL	See you tomorrow.	*Hasta mañana.*

CHAPTER 3
People—*La gente*

la abuela

la nieta

My Family—*Mi familia*

Now it's time to talk about family! Since you live with your family, you probably talk with them often and spend lots of time together. Perhaps your parents help you with your homework after school and take you to the park when the weather is nice. This chapter will teach you all you need to know to talk with your family in Spanish!

Every family is different. Some children live with their mother and father, while others only have one parent or live with a relative. The Spanish word for father is *el padre*, and the Spanish word for mother is *la madre*. Or you can call them *Papá* (dad) and *Mamá* (mom). Here are the Spanish words for other family members:

English	Spanish	English	Spanish
grandfather	*el abuelo*	boy cousin	*el primo*
grandmother	*la abuela*	girl cousin	*la prima*
husband	*el esposo*	nephew	*el sobrino*
wife	*la esposa*	niece	*la sobrina*
uncle	*el tío*	son	*el hijo*
aunt	*la tía*	daughter	*la hija*
brother	*el hermano*	grandson	*el nieto*
sister	*la hermana*	granddaughter	*la nieta*

Okay, it's time to practice these new words and see if you can remember what they mean. In the following section you'll be given a Spanish word for a family member. In the blank space, write the name of that person (or one of those people) in your family. So, for example, if you have a cousin named Michael, your response would look like this:

el primo   <u>   Michael   </u>

Consejo
IMPORTANT TIP

Did you notice that for every one of these family members, the Spanish words for boys and girls are the same except that the boy word ends in *o* and the girl word ends in *a*? When you look at it like that, it's like there are only half as many words to remember. If you know that a boy cousin is *el primo*, then it's easy to remember that a girl cousin is *la prima*.

Now try some on your own. If there is no one in your family with one of these titles, then just leave the space blank.

el tío	_____
la abuela	_____
la hermana	_____
el abuelo	_____
la prima	_____
el hermano	_____
la tía	_____

When you're talking about your family, there are a few other words you need to know. First is the verb *tener*, which means "to have." *Tengo* means "I have" and *tienes* means "you have." So you can ask your friend *¿Cuántos hermanos y hermanas tienes?* (How many brothers and sisters do you have?) and your friend might answer *Tengo dos hermanos y una hermana.* Now, answer this question about yourself: *¿Cuántos hermanos y hermanas tienes?* Don't forget to write the numbers in Spanish!

Yo tengo _____ hermanos y _____ hermanas.

The other useful words are "my" and "your." There are two words for each of those in Spanish. If you're talking about just one family member, you would use *mi* (my) or *tu* (your): *mi padre, mi madre* (my father, my mother), *tu padre, tu madre* (your father, your mother). If you're talking about more than one, you'll use *mis* (my) or *tus* (your): *mis hermanos, mis primos* (my brothers, my cousins), *tus hermanos, tus primos* (your brothers, your cousins).

Now you can talk to and about your family in Spanish! See what you can remember and go practice your new words with a parent or friend.

Diversión — Fun Stuff

Use all of your new Spanish vocabulary to make a family tree! To do this, start with yourself and branch out. Write your name and the word *yo*, which means "I" in Spanish. Then draw two lines branching out from you and write your parents' names plus *madre* and *padre*. Keep going until you've included aunts, uncles, cousins, grandparents, and anyone else you can think of! Be sure to show your family tree to your family when you're finished.

¡CUIDADO!
Mistake to Avoid

The Spanish word for "people" is *la gente*. If you want to say "one person," that would be *una persona*. And remember: The word *persona* is always feminine, whether that person is a man or a woman. So, for example, *tu padre* (your father) is *una persona*, too!

¿Cómo?— Say What?

You might have lots of friends, but you probably only have one best friend. In Spanish, a best friend is *el mejor amigo* or *la mejor amiga*. Here's a question for you: *¿Cómo se llama tu mejor amigo?* (What is your best friend's name?) Remember from Chapter 2, to answer you can say *Mi mejor amigo* (or *amiga*) *se llama* …. (My best friend's name is…)

More People—*Más gente*

Of course, there are lots more people in the world than just the ones in your family. Here are some other Spanish people words you should know:

English	Spanish
baby boy	*un niño*
baby girl	*una niña*
boy	*un chico*
	un muchacho
girl	*una chica*
	una muchacha
teenage boy	*un joven*
teenage girl	*una joven*
man	*un hombre*
woman	*una mujer*
boyfriend	*un novio*
girlfriend	*una novia*

In English, there are a lot of words for people that are the same whether the person is a boy or a girl. But in Spanish, there are two slightly different words for most people. Here are some common people words in English and their Spanish translations:

English	Spanish (male)	Spanish (female)
neighbor	*un vecino*	*una vecina*
teacher	*un profesor*	*una profesora*
student	*un estudiante*	*una estudiante*
friend	*un amigo*	*una amiga*
my best friend	*mi mejor amigo*	*mi mejor amiga*
enemy	*un enemigo*	*una enemiga*
driver	*un conductor*	*una conductora*
passenger	*un pasajero*	*una pasajera*

Descriptions and Personality—
Descripciones y personalidad

Now that you know what to call all of the different people you know, you can describe them. To ask "What is he or she like?" you can say *¿Cómo es?* or *¿Qué tal es?* In English, you might say, "He is tall" or "She is young." Here are some of these answers in Spanish:

bajo   alto

English	Spanish	English	Spanish
I am…	*Yo soy…*	thin	*delgado*
He is…	*Él es…*	young	*joven*
She is…	*Ella es…*	old	*viejo*
tall	*alto*	good-looking	*guapo*
short	*bajo*	ugly	*feo*
fat	*gordo*		

For example, *Él es bajo y delgado* means "He is short and thin." But what if you're describing a girl? In this case, you might need to change the ending of the word from o to a. For example, a tall girl is *alta*, and a pretty girl is *guapa*. The only word in this list that this doesn't work for is *joven*, which remains the same for a boy or a girl.

Now try describing yourself! For example:

I am young.   <u>Yo soy joven.</u>

Fill in the blanks to complete a sentence describing yourself:

Yo soy _____ y _____.

In English, the adjective (the describing word) comes before the noun; but it's the opposite in Spanish. When you speak Spanish, be sure to say the adjective after the noun.

Gramática —
Additional Grammar

If you're describing a girl, you would start with *Ella es* and then change the *o* at the end of the describing word to *a*: *Ella es alta* (she is tall), *ella es guapa* (she is pretty). If you're describing yourself, you would say *yo soy* and then the describing word ending with *o* if you're a boy and *a* if you're a girl. For example, *Yo soy bajo* (I'm short, for a boy) or *Yo soy guapa* (I'm pretty, for a girl).

So, for example, if a person has blue eyes, you would say she has *ojos azules* (eyes blue). To form a complete sentence, start with *él tiene* (he has) or *ella tiene* (she has), then *ojos* (eyes), then the color. Here are some examples:

English	Spanish
He has blue eyes.	*Él tiene ojos azules.*
She has green eyes.	*Ella tiene ojos verdes.*
Juan has gray eyes.	*Juan tiene ojos grises.*
Ana has brown eyes.	*Ana tiene ojos castaños.*

When you talk about someone's hair, it's just the same: *él tiene* or *ella tiene*, plus *cabello* or *pelo* (hair), and then the color or other description word. The words *pelo* and *cabello* both mean hair, so you can use whichever one you want. Here are some hair descriptions you can use:

English	Spanish
dark hair	*cabello/pelo oscuro*
black hair	*cabello/pelo negro*
brown hair	*cabello/pelo castaño*
red hair	*cabello/pelo rojo*
blond hair	*cabello/pelo rubio*
straight hair	*cabello/pelo liso*
curly hair	*cabello/pelo rizado*
wavy hair	*cabello/pelo ondulado*
short hair	*cabello/pelo corto*
long hair	*cabello/pelo largo*

What type of hair do you have? *Qué tipo de pelo tienes?* Fill in your answer here:

Yo tengo pelo _____ .

Two other words you might want to describe someone are *pecas* (freckles) and *hoyuelos* (dimples). For example:

English	Spanish
He has freckles.	*Él tiene pecas.*
She has dimples.	*Ella tiene hoyuelos.*

←las pecas

Now you know how to describe what everyone looks like, but what about their personality? For these descriptions, you'll use *Él es* or *Ella es*, plus the describing word. For the words that end in o, remember to change it to a for girls. If it doesn't end in o, then it's the same for boys and girls. Here are some adjectives you might use:

English	Spanish	English	Spanish
affectionate	*afectuoso*	outgoing	*abierto*
boring	*aburrido*	patient	*paciente*
brave	*valiente*	playful	*guasón*
friendly	*amistoso*	serious	*serio*
funny	*divertido*	shy	*tímido*
impatient	*impaciente*	smart	*inteligente*
interesting	*interesante*	snobbish	*esnob*
kind	*amable*	strong	*fuerte*
lazy	*perezoso*	studious	*estudioso*
mean	*mezquino*	stupid	*estúpido*
nice	*simpático*	weak	*débil*

fuerte

Do you have an affectionate friend (*un amigo afectuoso*)? An interesting aunt (*una tía interesante*)? Fill in the following blanks to complete sentences describing yourself and your family members. For yourself, you're going to use *Yo soy* again, which means I am. If you need to, refer back to the beginning of the chapter to review the Spanish words for different family members.

Yo soy _____ y _____.

Mi padre es _____ y _____.

Mi madre es _____ y _____.

Mi hermano es _____ y _____.

Mi hermana es _____ y _____.

Mi abuelo es _____ y _____.

Mi abuela es _____ y _____.

Mi tío es _____ y _____.

Mi tía es _____ y _____.

Mi primo es _____ y _____.

Mi prima es _____ y _____.

Consejo
IMPORTANT TIP

Remember that to ask how another person feels, you can just make a sentence with the *tú* form of the verb plus the adjective: *¿Estás triste?* (Are you sad?) Or you can use a question word: *¿Por qué estás enojado?* (Why are you angry?) To practice, try having a short conversation with someone in your family. Start by saying hello and asking how he or she feels in Spanish.

Feelings—*Sentimientos*

So now you know how to describe what people look like and what kind of personality they have, but what about how they feel? People's feelings change all the time, so you'll need to learn some new vocabulary to keep up with them.

For most feelings, you'll use the verb *estar* (to be). To say "I am" in Spanish, say *yo estoy.* To say "you are," say *tú eres.* Now, just add one of the following feelings words and you've got yourself a sentence!

English	Spanish
angry	*enojado*
annoyed	*enfadado*
bored	*aburrido*
depressed	*deprimido*

English	Spanish
dizzy	*mareado*
embarrassed	*avergonzado*
excited	*entusiasmado*
happy	*feliz, alegre*
jealous	*celoso*
nervous	*inquieto*
offended	*ofendido*
sad	*triste*
sick	*enfermo*
tired	*cansado*

When you feel bored, you can say *Estoy aburrido*. When you feel happy, you can say *Estoy feliz*. These are emotional feelings, which means they describe how your mind feels. For physical feelings (the way your body feels) you can't use *estar*; you need a different verb. This verb is *tener* (to have). In English, you say "I am hungry" or "I am cold," but in Spanish what you literally have to say is *Tengo hambre* (I have hunger) and *Tengo frío* (I have cold.) This may seem a little strange because of the way you are used to using "to have" in English. Don't worry; it just takes some getting used to.

To create a sentence using *tener*, start with *yo tengo* (I am) or *tú tienes* (you are). Then, add one of the following:

English	Spanish
hungry	*hambre*
thirsty	*sed*
hot	*calor*
cold	*frío*

To tell someone that you're hungry, you say, *Tengo hambre*. To ask someone if he or she is hot, just ask *¿Tienes calor?* Easy, right? Remember: Practice makes perfect!

> ## ¡CUIDADO!
> ### Mistake to Avoid
> Even though you should use *estar* with most emotional feeling words (like happy or sad) and *tener* with most physical feeling words (like hot or cold), some words don't follow these rules. For example, to say "I am scared" (an emotional feeling), you would say *Tengo miedo*.

Here's a great way to practice all the Spanish words for body parts: Draw a big picture of a person and label all of the different parts in Spanish. Don't forget all the details, like teeth and fingers. Once you've learned these body part words, you can label them all!

Consejo
IMPORTANT TIP

Did you notice that you use the same word to say both "finger" and "toe" in Spanish? The word *dedo* literally translates as "digit," which is another word you can use for finger and toe in English. If you need to be specific, you can say *dedo del pie*, so that the person you're talking to knows you mean your toe and not your finger. Now that you know how to say finger and toe in Spanish, practice the numbers you learned in Chapter 1 and try counting them: *Un dedo, dos dedos, tres dedos...* How high can you count?

Parts of the Body—*Partes del cuerpo*

Now it's time to learn how to talk about parts of your body. From your head to your toes, it's fun to describe all your parts in Spanish. Here are some good words to know:

English	Spanish
hair	*el cabello, el pelo*
head	*la cabeza*
face	*la cara*
eye	*el ojo*
nose	*la nariz*
cheek	*la mejilla*
mouth	*la boca*
lip	*el labio*
tooth	*el diente*
ear	*la oreja*

English	Spanish
neck	*el cuello*
chest	*el pecho*
back	*la espalda*
stomach	*el estómago*
arm	*el brazo*
shoulder	*el hombro*
elbow	*el codo*
wrist	*la muñeca*
hand	*la mano*
finger	*el dedo*
fingernail, toenail	*la uña*
thumb	*el pulgar*
leg	*la pierna*
knee	*la rodilla*
ankle	*el tobillo*
foot	*el pie*
toe	*el dedo*

la mano

Face to Face

These *niños* (children) are each missing something! Fill in the blanks with the correct English word and complete each picture.

I see ____ my _____.
Yo veo <u>con</u> mis <u>ojos</u>.

I smell _____ my _____.
Yo huelo <u>con</u> mi <u>nariz</u>.

I hear _____ my _____.
Yo oigo <u>con</u> mis <u>orejas</u>.

I eat _____ my _____.
Yo como <u>con</u> mi <u>boca</u>.

I taste _____ my _____.
Yo pruebo <u>con</u> mi <u>lengua</u>.

Clothes—*Ropa*

Wow, you've learned a lot of words to help you talk about the body so far. Now you just need to know how to talk about the clothes covering all those different parts of the body! Here are some words for clothes you probably have in your drawers and closet:

English	Spanish
bathing suit	*un traje de baño*
coat	*un abrigo*
jacket	*una chaqueta*
pajamas	*un pijama*
pants	*unos pantalones*
raincoat	*un impermeable*
shorts	*un short*
sweater	*un suéter*
T-shirt	*una camiseta*

Here are the Spanish words for some common boys' clothes:

English	Spanish
boxer shorts	*unos calzones*
shirt	*una camisa*
sports jacket	*una chaqueta sport*
suit	*un traje*
tie	*una corbata*
undershirt	*una camiseta*
underwear	*unos calzoncillos*

la camiseta

And here are the words for some girls' clothes:

English	Spanish
bikini	*un biquini*
blouse	*una blusa*
bra	*un sostén*
dress	*un vestido*
nightgown	*un camisón*
panties	*unas bragas*
skirt	*una falda*
tights	*unas pantimedias*

Of course, most people wear other things besides just clothing. You might also wear jewelry or other accessories. Perhaps you wear a belt or a pair of glasses. Here are the Spanish words for all these things:

English	Spanish
backpack	*una mochila*
belt	*un cinturón*
bracelet	*un brazalete*
earrings	*unos aretes*
glasses	*unas gafas*
gloves	*unos guantes*
hat	*un sombrero*
mittens	*unos mitones*
necklace	*un collar*
purse	*una bolsa*
ring	*un anillo*
scarf	*una bufanda*
sunglasses	*unas gafas de sol*
watch	*un reloj*
wallet	*una cartera*

**¿Cómo?—
Say What?**

The Spanish word for clothing is *la ropa* or *la prenda*. *Ropa* might make you think of "rope" but be careful! Those two words are called "false friends," meaning that they look similar but mean different things. There are lots of "false friends" in English and Spanish. You'll learn more later in the book.

Here are some things you might wear on your feet:

English	Spanish
boots	*unas botas*
high-heeled shoes	*unos zapatos de tacones altos*
sandals	*unas sandalias*
shoes	*unos zapatos*
slippers	*unas zapatillas*
sneakers	*unos deportivos*
socks	*unos calcetines*

In English, you would use the word "wear" to tell someone what you're wearing, weather it's a shirt or a pair of shoes. But this is different in Spanish! The Spanish verb "to wear" is *llevar* for clothing and *calzar* for shoes. So, here's an example:

English	Spanish
I'm wearing shorts and a T-shirt and sandals.	*Llevo unos pantalones cortos y una camiseta y calzo unas sandalias.*

Now try describing the outfit you have on today. Fill in the blanks to create a complete sentence:

Llevo _____ *y* _____ *y calzo* _____.

To describe what someone else is wearing use the word *Lleva*, which means "He (or She) is wearing." For example, if your mother is wearing a dress and a necklace, you would say *Lleva un vestido y un collar*. Keep creating new sentences using all the new words you learned in this chapter. Remember: The more you practice, the easier it will be!

CHAPTER 4
Places and Things
Lugares y cosas

All Around Town

Find your way through the maze to learn the Spanish words for these familiar places! Start at the picture described in question number one. Find your way to the rest of the pictures. Write both the English and Spanish words on the lines provided.

1. Where do you borrow books?
2. Where do you study?
3 Where do you play?
4. Where do you mail a letter?
5. Where do you shop for food?

1. _____

2. _____

3. _____

4. _____

5. _____

Shopping and Errands—*Compras y mandados*

There are all kinds of different stores and other places you might need to go to get your shopping and other errands done. Shopping for food can require a lot of different stops. Here are some places you might go to get the groceries you need:

English	Spanish
bakery	*la panadería*
butcher	*la carnicería*
candy store	*la confitería*
fruit stand	*la frutería*
grocery store	*la tienda de comestibles*
market	*el mercado*
supermarket	*el supermercado*

Here are some sentences you might use when talking about shopping for food:

English	Spanish
I'm going to the bakery.	*Voy a la panadería.*
Let's go to the candy store.	*Vamos a la confitería.*

There are also lots of other places you might need to visit. Here are some examples:

English	Spanish
bank	*el banco*
barber	*la barbería*
beauty shop	*la peluquería*
church	*la iglesia*
clothing store	*la ropería*
department store	*los grandes almacenes, las tiendas por departamentos*

¡CUIDADO!
Mistake to Avoid

What's the difference between a grocery store, a market, and a supermarket? Well, a supermarket is a huge store that sells all kinds of fresh, boxed, and canned food, plus has special sections like a deli counter and bakery. A grocery store is a small, local store that sells food and things, and a market usually sells food outside, like a stand at a farmer's market.

Do you know where the post office is in your town? The library? The school? Draw a map of your town and label in Spanish all the different buildings. If your town doesn't have all of the places on the list, you can make some up!

English	Spanish
dentist	el dentista
doctor	el médico
dry cleaner	la tintorería
eye doctor	el oftalmólogo
hardware store	la ferretería
laundromat	la lavandería
library	la biblioteca
pharmacy	la farmacia
post office	la oficina de correos
stationery store	la papelería

Transportation—*Transporte*

Now that you know where you're going, you just need to figure out how to get there! This is where transporation comes in. Transportation includes all the vehicles that take you places, like cars, buses, and bicycles.

With all of these different methods of transportation, you're going to use a new verb: *ir* (to go). The conjugations you might need for this verb are *yo voy* (I go), *tú vas* (you go), and *nosotros vamos* (we go). After the verb, you're going to use *en*, which means "in" or "by." For example:

English	Spanish
I'm going by car.	*Yo voy en coche*
Are you going by train?	*¿Vas en tren?*
We're going in a plane.	*Nosotros vamos en avión.*

For walking, though, you don't use *en*. You use *a* instead:

English	Spanish
I'm walking.	*Voy a pie.*

Here are some common modes of transportation you might use to get where you need to go:

English	Spanish
bicycle	*la bicicleta*
boat	*el barco*
bus	*el autobús*
car	*el coche*
ferry	*el transbordador*
helicopter	*el helicóptero*
jet ski	*la moto acuática*
motorbike	*la moto*
motorboat	*la lancha a motor*
motorcycle	*la motocicleta*
plane	*el avión*
RV	*la caravana pequeña*
sailboat	*el barco de vela*
scooter	*el scooter, el ciclomotor*
skateboard	*el monopatín*
skates	*los patines*
subway	*el metro*
taxi	*el taxi*
train	*el tren*
tricycle	*el triciclo*
truck	*el camión*
van	*la camioneta*
walking	*a pie*

el autobús

**¿Cómo?—
Say What?**

In a discussion about transportation, you might also need to use some other words. Perhaps you have to buy a bus or train ticket before you can board. Here are some words that will help you: station—*la estación*, ticket—*el billete*, to buy—*comprar*, to pay—*pagar*.

Vacation—*Vacaciones*

Where do you like to go on vacation? The beach? The mountains? Around the world? Here is some Spanish vocabulary to help you find your way there—and back home.

Consejo
IMPORTANT TIP

If you're going to another country, there are a few extra words you'll need to know: customs—*la aduana*; immigration—*la inmigración*; passport—*el pasaporte*; visa—*un visado/una visa*.

English	Spanish
Where are you going?	*¿Adónde vas?*
I'm going…	*Voy…*
to an amusement park	*a un parque de atracciones*
to my grandparents' house	*a la casa de mis abuelos*
to the beach	*a la playa*
to the city	*a la ciudad*
to the mountains	*a las montañas*
to the rainforest	*al bosque tropical*
overseas	*al extranjero*

Here are a couple of examples:

English	Spanish
I'm going to the beach.	*Voy a la playa.*
I'm going overseas.	*Voy al extranjero.*

When you travel long distances, you sometimes have to fly in an airplane. Here's some vocabulary to use at the airport:

English	Spanish
airport	*el aeropuerto*
Arrivals	*Llegadas*
baggage	*el equipaje*
baggage claim	*el reclamo de equipaje*
boarding pass	*la tarjeta de embarque*
carry-on luggage	*el equipaje de mano*
checked luggage	*el equipaje registrado*
check-in desk	*el mostrador de registro*
Departures	*Salidas*
economy (coach) class	*la clase económica*
first class	*la primera clase*
flight	*un vuelo*

English	Spanish
gate	*una puerta*
layover	*una escala*
one-way ticket	*un billete sencillo*
plane ticket	*un billete de avión*
round-trip ticket	*un billete de ida y vuelta*
security check	*el control de seguridad*
shuttle	*un servicio de autobús*
terminal	*la terminal*

Here are some verbs to use at the airport:

English	Spanish
to board	*embarcar*
to buy a ticket	*comprar un billete*
to land	*aterrizar*
to make a reservation	*hacer una reservación*
to take off	*despegar*

Once you've arrived at your destination, you can help your parents or other family members by knowing the following helpful words and phrases:

English	Spanish
Where is the...?	*¿Dónde está...?*
bank	*el banco*
bathroom	*el baño*
church	*la iglesia*
currency exchange	*el cambio de moneda*
hospital	*el hospital*
hotel	*el hotel*
movie theater	*el cine*
museum	*el museo*
park	*el parque*
police station	*la comisaría*

Gotta Go!

You have just traveled a long way, and you need to go—quick! Use the directions to cross out words in the grid. Read the leftover words from top to bottom and left to right. That's the polite way to ask directions to the bathroom!

Cross out: *números* • *familia* • *colores*

Can you add the correct punctuation? Remember to think upside-down!

UNO	DÓNDE	EL HIJO
ESTÁ	PAPÁ	OCHO
ROJO	EL	AZUL
LA TÍA	SEIS	BAÑO
POR	VERDE	FAVOR

la escuela

English	Spanish
pool	*la piscina*
post office	*la oficina de correos*
restaurant	*el restaurante*
school	*la escuela*
theater	*el teatro*

Now pretend that you're at your vacation destination and you need to ask where some different places are. Remember the words and phrases you just learned and complete some sentences asking where different places are. For example, if you want to know where the post office is, you would ask *¿Dónde está la oficina de correos?* Try it out:

¿Dónde está? _____

¿Dónde está? _____

¿Dónde está? _____

¿Dónde está? _____

¿Dónde está? _____

When you and your family are trying to get somewhere, you'll also need to talk about directions and locations. For instance, you might need to go through the door on the left, visit the counter in front of the escalator, or travel west on the highway. Here are some words that will help you talk about direction and location:

English	Spanish
It is...	*Está...*
To the left	*a la izquierda*
To the right	*a la derecha*
straight ahead	*todo seguido*

¡CUIDADO!
Mistake to Avoid

The Spanish words for "east" and "west" are kind of similar, so be sure to pronounce them correctly. *Este* (east) is pronounced ES teh, and *oeste* (west) is pronounced oh ES teh—don't forget to say that *o* at the beginning, which is pronounced like "oh"!

English	Spanish
next to	*junto a*
in front of	*enfrente de*
in back of	*detrás de*
up	*arriba*
down	*abajo*
near	*cerca*
far	*lejos*
north	*norte*
south	*sur*
east	*este*
west	*oeste*

norte

oeste   *este*

sur

Colors—*Colores*

Now it's time to talk about colors! Knowing how to say all the colors in Spanish will help you describe the things you see. Perhaps there is a blue mailbox down the street or a red bird in the tree. Once you know all these words, you can describe almost anything!

English	Spanish
red	*rojo*
purple	*violeta*
blue	*azul*
green	*verde*
yellow	*amarillo*
orange	*anaranjado*
black	*negro*
white	*blanco*
gray	*gris*
brown	*marrón*
pink	*rosado*

Diversión—Fun Stuff

Write the Spanish words for all the colors on small stickers and use them to label your crayons, pens, markers, and paints. This will help you remember these new words!

One important difference in Spanish is that adjectives like colors come after the noun, instead of before it, like in English. In the following examples, notice how the color comes before the noun in English but after it in Spanish:

English	Spanish
My mom has a blue car.	*Mi mamá tiene un coche blanco.*
I have a purple bike.	*Tengo una bicicleta violeta.*

Do you see how the word *violeta* was used to describe *bicicleta*? This is because *bicicleta* is a feminine word (it ends in *a*). Remember to change the ending to *a* if the word you're describing is feminine.

Now use the Spanish words for colors to describe some of the different things you have. These are all words you've already learned, so you just have to remember what they mean and then add a color in the blank space. Remember to change the ending on the color word to match the gender of the word your describing, if necessary.

Gramática —
Additional Grammar

To describe a color as "light" or "dark," you need to know the words *claro* (light) and *oscuro* (dark). For example: light gray—*gris claro*; light green—*verde claro*; dark red—*rojo oscuro*; dark purple—*violeta oscuro*.

una bicicleta _____

una mochila _____

un suéter _____

una camiseta _____

Now that you know how to talk about colors in Spanish, go tell your family what your favorite color is. Start with *Mi color favorito es* and then add the color. So, if your favorite color is red, just say *Mi color favorito es el rojo*. It's easy!

Shapes—*Formas*

Now you know how to describe things by their color, but what about their shape? Circles, ovals, and triangles are common shapes. Here are some shape words to help you describe what you see around you:

English	Spanish
arch	*un arco*
circle	*un círculo*
cone	*un cono*
crescent	*una media luna*
cube	*un cubo*
curve	*una curva*
cylinder	*un cilindro*
diamond	*un diamante*
heart	*un corazón*
hexagon	*un hexágono*
line	*una línea*
octagon	*un octágono*
oval	*un óvalo*
pentagon	*un pentágono*
pyramid	*una pirámide*
rectangle	*un rectángulo*
sphere	*una esfera*
square	*un cuadrado*
star	*una estrella*
triangle	*un triángulo*

Sizes—*Tamaños*

While color and shape are good ways to describe things, you can also talk about size. Here are some good size words to know:

¿Cómo?— Say What?

Did you know that there are different categories of shapes? Shapes like circles and squares are two-dimensional, *bidimensional*, which means they're flat. Shapes like spheres and cubes are three-dimensional (3-D), *tridimensional*, so you can actually hold them in your hand and see all their sides.

Diversión—Fun Stuff

Don't forget the best shape of all! The Spanish word for "rainbow" is *arco iris*. Draw a rainbow and label each stripe with the Spanish word for that color. ROY G. BIV is a trick to help you remember the colors: red, orange, yellow, green, blue, indigo (dark blue), and violet.

Gramática —
Additional Grammar

To say that something is more ____, or that it's ____-er than something else, you use the word *más* (more) in Spanish. For example, to say "The dog is bigger than the cat," say *El perro es más grande que el gato*. To say, "I want a smaller book," say, *Quiero un libro más pequeño*.

Consejo
IMPORTANT TIP

There are other quantity words that are less specific but just as useful: *mucho* (a lot), *muchísimo* (a whole lot), *un poquito* (a little), *una miaja* (a tiny bit), *más* (more), and *menos* (less).

English	Spanish
huge	*enorme*
large	*grande*
long	*largo*
medium	*mediano*
narrow	*estrecho*
short	*corto*
small	*pequeño*
tiny	*pequeñito*
wide	*ancho*

In Spanish, not only are there different words for weights and distances, but there is also a different system of measurement. Americans use the "English system," which includes inches, feet, miles, pounds, gallons, etc. Most of the rest of the world uses the "metric system."

To measure distance, the metric system uses "meters." One meter (*un metro*) is a little more than three feet. One kilometer (a thousand meters) is just over half a mile. A centimeter is one hundredth of a meter; 2½ centimeters equal one inch.

For weight, the metric system uses "grams." Thirty-two grams (*gramos*) equal about an ounce. A kilogram (1,000 grams) equals 2.2 pounds.

The metric system measures volume with "liters." One liter (*un litro*) is a bit more than a quart.

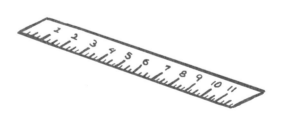

CHAPTER 5

At Home
En la casa

Rooms and Furniture—*Cuartos y muebles*

When you're at home—*en la casa*—you can use this Spanish vocabulary to explain where you are and what your house is like. Here are rooms and other places and things you might find in your home:

English	Spanish
attic	*el desván*
balcony	*el balcón*
basement	*el sótano*
bathroom	*el baño*
bedroom	*el dormitorio*
ceiling	*el techo*
den	*el salón*
dining room	*el comedor*
door	*la puerta*
floor	*el piso*
hall	*el pasillo*
kitchen	*la cocina*
porch	*la veranda*
room	*el cuarto, la pieza*
screen door	*la puerta con mosquitera*
stairway	*la escalera*
study	*el despacho*
wall	*la pared*
window	*la ventana*

Once you know what all of the different rooms and spaces are called, you can fill them up with furniture and other things.

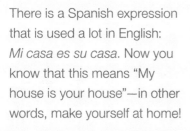

¿Cómo?— Say What?

There is a Spanish expression that is used a lot in English: *Mi casa es su casa*. Now you know that this means "My house is your house"—in other words, make yourself at home!

English	Spanish
bookshelf	*una estantería*
carpet	*una moqueta*
chair	*una silla*
computer	*una computadora*
couch	*un sofá*
curtain	*una cortina*
desk	*un escritorio*
dryer	*una secadora*
lamp	*una lámpara*
poster	*un cartel*
printer	*una impresora*
rug	*un tapete, una alfombra*
stereo	*un estéreo*
table	*una mesa*
telephone	*un teléfono*
television	*una televisión*
washer	*una lavadora*

el teléfono

Here are some things found in the bathroom:

English	Spanish
bathtub	*una bañera, un baño*
mirror	*un espejo*
shower	*una ducha*
sink	*un lavabo*

Here's what you might find in the bedroom:

English	Spanish
alarm clock	*un despertador*
bed	*una cama*
closet	*un clóset, un armario empotrado*
dresser	*un tocador*

Diversión_Fun Stuff

Want a fun way to practice your house vocabulary? Draw a big picture of your house and label all of the rooms, spaces, and furniture with their Spanish names. Keep adding to your picture as you learn more words later in this chapter.

My Room

If your bedroom had a large, blank *pared* (wall), what could you use to decorate it? Use the decoder to find out! Extra fun: Use brightly colored markers to write the answer letters on top of the coded letters. Then turn the letters into the kind of wall decoration this puzzle is about!

UN

CARTEL

A = O
C = P
E = E
L = R
UN = A
R = S
T = T

What else does this boy have in his room? Collect the letters in order from *uno* to *siete* and find out!

el fútbol

6 M
3 A
1 U
4 C
7 A
R
J N A
2
5

In the Kitchen—*En la cocina*

The kitchen has a lot of different things in it. How many of these can you find in your kitchen?

English	Spanish
bottle	una botella
bowl	un bol
box	una caja
can	una lata
cookie sheet	una bandeja de horno
cup	una taza
dishwasher	una lavavajillas
fork	un tenedor
frying pan	una sartén
glass	un vaso
jar	un pote
knife	un cuchillo
napkin	una servilleta
oven	un horno
plate	un plato
pot	una cazuela, una olla
refrigerator	un refrigerador, una nevera
saucer	un platillo
sink	un fregadero
spatula	una espátula
spoon	una cuchara
stove	una estufa, una cocina
whisk	un batidor
wooden spoon	una cuchara de madera

Consejo
IMPORTANT TIP

Be careful about the word *vaso*, which means "glass." Don't let *vaso* fool you into thinking it means "vase"—that's called *un florero* in Spanish. These are false friends!

Gramática —
Additional Grammar

In Spanish, the word ending *-illo* means little. So *un plato* is a plate, and *un platillo* is a little plate—or a saucer!

Now see if you can remember what all these kitchen words mean! Use the following checklist to find all these items in your kitchen. As you find each one, write a checkmark in the box next to it. You'll have to recognize the Spanish words, so this may be a little tricky!

☐ un tenedor
☐ un bol
☐ una lata
☐ una taza
☐ una sartén
☐ un fregadero
☐ un pote
☐ un cuchillo
☐ un plato
☐ una cuchara

el plato

Outside—*Afuera*

You might have lots of different things outside your house too, like a yard, sidewalk, or driveway. Use this vocabulary to explain what the outside of your house is like in Spanish.

English	Spanish
clothesline	la cuerda para la ropa
doghouse	la caseta del perro
driveway	la entrada
fence	la valla
flower	la flor
garage	el garaje
garden	el jardín
gate	la verja

hammock	*la hamaca*
hose	*la manguera*
mailbox	*el buzón*
parking space	*el aparcamiento*
path	*el camino*
patio	*el patio*
road	*la calle*
sandbox	*el cajón de arena*
sidewalk	*la acera*
slide	*el tobogán*
swing	*el columpio*
trail	*la pista*
tree	*el árbol*
yard	*el jardín*

el árbol

Go outside and see which of these items are in your yard. Look all around the yard and write down the Spanish words for the different things you find in the following blank spaces:

_____

_____

_____

_____

_____

Everyday Actions—*Todos los días*

There are some things that you do every day, or almost every day, so you need to be able to talk about that stuff, too.

English	Spanish
to wake up	*despertarse*
to get up	*levantarse*
to get tired	*cansarse*
to go to bed	*acostarse*
to fall asleep	*dormirse*
to get ready	*arreglarse*
to take a bath	*bañarse*
to take a shower	*ducharse*
to wash (up)	*lavarse*
to get dressed	*vestirse*
to put on clothes	*ponerse*
to brush (hair, teeth)	*cepillarse*
to comb (hair)	*peinarse*
to take off clothes	*quitarse*

A verb with *se* at the end is a reflexive verb. This means that it needs an extra word when you conjugate it. So for *cansarse*, you would say *Yo me canso* (I'm getting tired) and *¿Tú te cansas?* (Are you getting tired)?

Here are some sample sentences using reflexive verbs:

English	Spanish
I'm washing up.	*Me lavo.*
I'm taking a bath.	*Me baño.*
I'm brushing my teeth.	*Me cepillo los dientes.*

Consejo
IMPORTANT TIP

Here are a couple of extra verbs to describe what your parents might do every day: to put on makeup—*maquillarse, pintarse*; to shave—*afeitarse*.

Chores—*Quehaceres domésticos*

Don't forget to do your chores! Here are some chore verbs that will come in handy as you and your family are taking care of things around the house:

English	Spanish
to cook	*cocinar*
to do laundry	*lavar la ropa*
to do the dishes	*lavar los platos*
to do the shopping	*hacer las compras*
to make the bed	*hacer la cama*
to mop the floor	*fregar el suelo*
to mow the lawn	*cortar el césped*
to put the house in order	*arreglar la casa*
to straighten up	*poner en orden*
to sweep the floor	*barrer el suelo*
to take out the garbage	*sacar la basura*
to vacuum	*pasar la aspiradora*

> ### Gramática —
> **Additional Grammar**
>
> To say that you have to do a certain chore, use *Tengo que* plus that expression. For example, if you have to do the dishes, you would say *Tengo que lavar los platos*.

Chores aren't always very fun, are they? Well, here's a way to make chores more interesting: Make a list of the chores that you have to do, but in Spanish! Fill in the following blanks to create a complete chore list. Your parents will be so impressed with your Spanish and your hard work!

1. _____

2. _____

3. _____

4. _____

5. _____

Pets—*Animales domésticos*

A good pet can be like a member of the family, so be sure you know the word for your pet in Spanish. Here are some types of pets and their Spanish translations:

> ### ¡CUIDADO!
> **Mistake to Avoid**
>
> *Rata* and *ratón* both look like they could mean "rat," so you need to make a special effort to remember that *ratón* means mouse, as in *el Ratón Mickey* (Mickey Mouse). *Rata* is actually the word for rat in Spanish.

el gato

English	Spanish
ant	una hormiga
bird	un pájaro
cat	un gato
dog	un perro
ferret	un hurón
fish	un pez
frog	una rana
gerbil	un gerbo
guinea-pig	un cobayo
hamster	un hámster
hermit crab	un cangrejo ermitaño
horse	un caballo
mouse	un ratón
rabbit	un conejo
rat	una rata
snake	una serpiente
tarantula	una tarántula
turtle	una tortuga

Do you already have a pet? If so, what kind? Write a complete sentence saying what kind of pet you have. You'll start with the word *Tengo*, which means I have. For example, "I have a turtle" is *Tengo una torguga* in Spanish.

Tengo _____ .

If you don't already have a pet, do you want one? To say that you want something, you start with *Quiero*. So, to say "I want a dog," you would say, *Quiero un perro*. Use the following to complete such a sentence:

Quiero _____ .

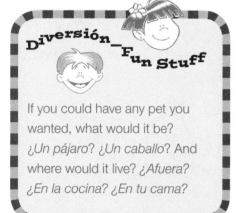

D**iversión**—F**un Stuff**

If you could have any pet you wanted, what would it be? *¿Un pájaro? ¿Un caballo?* And where would it live? *¿Afuera? ¿En la cocina? ¿En tu cama?*

CHAPTER 6

School and Work
Escuela y trabajo

¿Cómo?— Say What?

Even though the word *mapa* ends in *a,* it's masculine, not feminine. There are a few other words like this as well, including *un día* (day), *un problema* (problem), and *un programa* (program). You have to make an extra effort to remember these words that don't follow the rule!

Diversión—Fun Stuff

Chances are, one of your favorite times of the day is probably recess, which is called *el recreo* in Spanish, and a playground is *un patio de recreo*. Some things you might find in a playground are *un columpio* (swing), *un tobogán* (slide), *un cajón de arena* (sandbox), and *una trepadora* (jungle gym),

At School—*En la escuela*

Right now, your job is to go to school. You probably learn about all different subjects at school and use lots of different tools to do your work. Here are some Spanish words to help you talk about your job as a student.

English	Spanish
school	*una escuela*
high school	*una escuela secundaria*
college	*una universidad*
backpack	*una mochila*
calculator	*una calculadora*
chalk	*una tiza*
chalkboard	*una pizarra*
class	*una clase*
classroom	*un aula*
crayons	*lápices de color*
desk	*un pupitre*
glue	*una cola*
homework	*una tarea*
map	*un mapa*
notebook	*un cuaderno*
ruler	*una regla*
scissors	*unas tijeras*
tape	*una cinta adhesiva*
test	*un examen*
quiz	*una prueba*

las tijeras

Classes—*Clases*

Your job as a student can include all kinds of interesting classes. Here are some of the subjects you might be studying.

English	Spanish
art	*el arte*
biology	*la biología*
chemistry	*la química*
civics	*la educación cívica*
English	*el inglés*
French	*el francés*
geography	*la geografía*
German	*el alemán*
gym, physical education	*la educación física*
history	*la historia*
home economics	*la ciencia del hogar*
Latin	*el latín*
math	*las matemáticas*
music	*la música*
science	*la ciencia*
social studies	*los estudios sociales*
Spanish	*el español*

Gramática — Additional Grammar

All of the words for different languages are masculine, so that's easy. The hard part is that there are two Spanish words that mean language in general, and one is masculine and one is feminine: *el idioma* and *la lengua*.

You probably like some classes in school more than others, right? What is your favorite class? To answer this question in Spanish, you would say *Mi clase favorita es*... Give it a try:

Mi clase favorita es _____ .

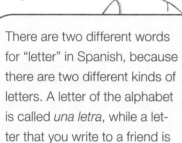

There are two different words for "letter" in Spanish, because there are two different kinds of letters. A letter of the alphabet is called *una letra*, while a letter that you write to a friend is called *una carta*.

Reading and Writing—*Lectura y escritura*

Reading and writing are two things that you have to do in almost all of your classes. Here are some of the things you'll need.

English	Spanish
book	*un libro*
dictionary	*un diccionario*
eraser	*un borrador*
paper	*el papel*
pen	*una pluma*
pencil	*un lápiz*
reading	*la lectura*
to read	*leer*
spelling	*la ortografía*
How do you spell ____?	*¿Cómo se escribe ____?*
writing	*la escritura*
to write	*escribir*
to write in cursive	*escribir en cursiva*
accent	*un acento*

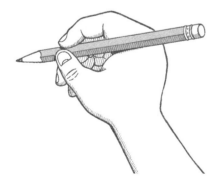

Consejo
IMPORTANT TIP

Papel refers to paper in general, like if you want to say "I don't have any paper" (*No tengo papel*). When you want to talk about a piece of paper, you would say *una hoja de papel* or *un trozo de papel*. For example, "I need a piece of paper" would be *Necesito una hoja de papel*. Another interesting fact is that the word *hoja* means leaf, so when you say *una hoja de papel*, you're literally saying a leaf of paper. This is what the term "loose-leaf" paper refers to!

Reading List

Use the clues to fill a letter into each empty box. When you are done, you'll have a Spanish word that answers this silly riddle:

What do all students need to read?

☐	letter right after T
☐	letter just before O
☐	letter between K and M
☐	the ninth letter
☐	the second letter
☐	the second letter after P
☐	letter right after N

On the Computer—*En la computadora*

You probably do a lot of work (and play) on the computer. Here is the Spanish vocabulary you need to talk about the computer:

English	Spanish
CD-ROM	*un CD-ROM*
computer	*una computadora*
database	*una base de datos*
disk drive	*una unidad de disco*
file	*un fichero*
hard drive	*un disco duro*
hardware	*un hardware*
keyboard	*un teclado*
laptop (computer)	*una computadora portátil*
monitor	*un monitor*
mouse	*un ratón*
to print	*imprimir*

English	Spanish
printer	*una impresora*
to save	*archivar*
software	*el software*
spell checker	*el corrector ortográfico*
to type	*escribir a máquina*
word processor	*un procesador de textos*
video game	*un videojuego*

And of course what would a computer be without the Internet and e-mail?

English	Spanish
e-mail	*el correo electrónico*
e-mail address	*la dirección electrónica*
Internet	*el Internet*
Internet browser	*un navegador*
Internet café	*un cibercafé*
search engine	*un motor de búsqueda*
Web page	*una página Web*
Web site	*un sitio Web*

Jobs—*Trabajos*

Right now your job is to go to school, but when you grow up, you'll have a different job. Perhaps you've thought about becoming a firefighter or a pilot. Here are the Spanish words for some cool careers:

English	Spanish
actor/actress	*un actor/una actriz*
artist	*un/una artista*
baker	*un panadero/una panadera*

Diversión—Fun Stuff

If you don't have an e-mail address and would like to create one, or if you have one and would like to change it, why not try making one in Spanish? For example, if you like cats, you might create an address like *gatos123@yahoo.com.* If you like the color blue, you might choose *azul_is_cool@hotmail.com.* Ask your parent for help when you do this.

English	Spanish
butcher	*un carnicero, una carnicera*
carpenter	*un carpintero, una carpintera*
cashier	*un cajero, una cajera*
cook	*un cocinero, una cocinera*
doctor	*un doctor, una doctora*
electrician	*un/una electricista*
employee	*un empleado, una empleada*
engineer	*un ingeniero, una ingeniera*
fireman	*un bombero, una bombera*
flight attendant	*un/una auxiliar de vuelo*
lawyer	*un abogado, una abogada*
maid	*una criada*
mail carrier	*un cartero, una cartera*
manager	*un/una gerente*
mechanic	*un mecánico, una mecánica*
nurse	*un enfermero, una enfermera*
pilot	*un/una piloto*
plumber	*un plomero, una plomera*
police officer	*un/una policía*
receptionist	*un/una recepcionista*
secretary	*un secretario, una secretaria*
student	*un/una estudiante*
teacher	*un profesor, una profesora*
waiter/waitress	*un camarero, una camerera*
writer	*un escritor, una escritora*

Consejo
IMPORTANT TIP

When talking about most jobs, you have to explain whether the person is a man or a woman. Sometimes the word itself is the same; for example, *piloto* is the same for men and women. But the article always shows the difference: *un piloto* (man) and *una piloto* (woman).

Dressed for Work

What is *el bombero* (the fireman) wearing to work? Going from left to right, cross out the letters that spell the English word for each thing. Color the leftover letters to learn the Spanish word!

EL **HCEALSMCEOT**

EL **ACBROIGAOT**

LOS **GGULAONVTESES**

LOS **PPAANNTTALONESS**

LAS **BBOOOTTASS**

EXTRA FUN: Who is the fireman's friend?

EL **DPEORRGO**

At the Office—*En la oficina*

Many people work in offices, so this last section on jobs includes lots of vocabulary to help you find your way around the office.

English	Spanish
briefcase	*un maletín*
calculator	*una calculadora*
chair	*una silla*
copy machine	*una copiadora*
desk	*un escritorio*
fax machine	*un fax*
file folder	*una carpeta*
filing cabinet	*un fichero*
highlighter	*un marcador*
index card	*una ficha*
mail	*el correo*
office	*una oficina*
paper clip	*un clip*
rubber band	*una goma*
staple	*una grapa*
stapler	*una grapadora*
telephone	*un teléfono*
typewriter	*una máquina de escribir*

¿Cómo?— Say What?

Remember *un pupitre* from the section on school? That's a special kind of desk found in classrooms. But a regular desk, like adults use, is called *un escritorio*.

¡CUIDADO!
Mistake to Avoid

Be careful with *carpeta* and *grapa*—they don't mean "carpet" and "grape," but rather "folder" and "staple." These are just two of many "false friends" in English and Spanish.

Did you know that some people do their work from home? Maybe you have a parent who does this from an office right in your house. Whether your parents work at home or someplace else, chances are you have some office supplies in different places in your house. Let's take a look around!

The following list contains the Spanish words for different office supplies. If you can't remember what a word means, you can look back at the vocabulary lists that appear earlier in this chapter. Search around your house until you find each of the items in the list. Then, fill in the blank spaces with the room or rooms where you found each item and how many you found. Here's the tricky part: You must write down the rooms and the numbers in Spanish! Go back to Chapter 5 if you're having trouble remembering how to say the different rooms in Spanish. The first one is done as an example.

Item in Spanish	Location(s)	Number of Items Found
un teléfono	la cocina	uno
una goma		
una grapa		
un clip		
un ratón		
una grapadora		
una pluma		
una ficha		
un marcador		
unas tijeras		
una calculadora		
una computadora		

CHAPTER 7
Time and Dates
Hora y fechas

Son las tres y media

What Time Is It?—*¿Qué hora es?*

Telling time in Spanish is very easy, as long as you know your numbers. Good thing you're a numbers expert since reading Chapter 1, right? If you need to refresh your memory, go back and revisit that part of the book for a few minutes.

To ask what time it is, just say *¿Qué hora es?* Then to answer, you say *son las* and then the number. Here are some example answers:

English	Spanish
It's two o'clock.	*Son las dos.*
It's three o'clock.	*Son las tres.*

To say that it's something thirty, use *media* (half).

English	Spanish
It's 3:30.	*Son las tres y media.*
It's 4:30.	*Son las cuatro y media.*

When you're talking about time the word "quarter" means a span of fifteen minutes. To say that it's quarter after or quarter to in Spanish, use y *cuarto* (quarter after) or *menos cuarto* (quarter to).

English	Spanish
It's 5:15.	*Son las cinco y cuarto.*
It's 6:15.	*Son las seis y cuarto.*
It's 6:45.	*Son las siete menos cuarto.*
It's 7:45.	*Son las ocho menos cuarto.*

For other times, like ten after and five to, you'll use either *y* (if it's time added on to the hour) or *menos* (if it's time substracted from the hour), plus the the number.

English	Spanish
It's 8:10.	*Son las ocho y diez.*
It's 9:20.	*Son las nueve y veinte.*
It's 10:55.	*Son las once menos cinco.*
It's 11:40.	*Son las doce menos veinte.*

Talking about "A.M." and "P.M." is a little different in Spanish. For A.M., you can use *de la mañana* (in the morning): *Son las seis de la mañana* (It's six A.M.) But for P.M., you have two choices: *de la tarde* (in the afternoon), when talking about anywhere from noon to about 6 P.M., and *de la noche* (in the evening or at night), for 6 P.M. to midnight. Here are some examples:

English	Spanish
It's one P.M. It's one in the afternoon.	*Es la una de la tarde.*
It's seven P.M. It's seven in the evening.	*Son las seis de la noche.*
It's eleven P.M. It's eleven at night.	*Son las once de la noche.*

Schedules, such as for buses and trains, often talk about time using a 24-hour clock. 1 A.M. to 12 noon are easy enough, and then after that, you just continue counting up: 1 P.M. = 13, 2 P.M. = 14, etc., all the way up to midnight — 24.

Consejo
IMPORTANT TIP

There are three occasions where you use *es* instead of *son* when you're talking about time: It's one o'clock—*Es la una.* It's noon—*Es mediodía.* It's midnight—*Es medianoche.* Also, if you want to say that something will be happening at a certain time, you use the word *a*, which means "at" in Spanish. For example, "at seven o'clock" is *a las siete.*

Days, months, and seasons—
Días, meses y estaciones

The Spanish days of the week are very different from the English ones:

English	Spanish
Monday	*lunes*
Tuesday	*martes*
Wednesday	*miércoles*
Thursday	*jueves*
Friday	*viernes*
Saturday	*sábado*
Sunday	*domingo*

¿Cómo?— Say What?

The Spanish week starts on Monday instead of Sunday. In addition, days of the week are not capitalized in Spanish the way they are in English.

Now that you know how to tell time and say the days of the week in Spanish, it's time to practice what you've learned. Make a schedule of your typical day, with the times and everything you do written in Spanish. For example, you might list waking up in the morning, eating breakfast, and taking a shower before school. Revisit the section called Everyday Actions—*Todos los días* in Chapter 5 if you need help remembering how to say certain daily activities. Here's a sample of what one entry in your schedule might look like:

El día (day)	*La hora* (time)	*La actividad* (activity)
lunes	*a las siete de la mañana*	*despertarse*

Here are the words for the months of the year — *los meses del año*:

English	Spanish
January	*enero*
February	*febrero*
March	*marzo*
April	*abril*
May	*mayo*
June	*junio*
July	*julio*
August	*agosto*
September	*septiembre*
October	*octubre*
November	*noviembre*
December	*diciembre*

¡CUIDADO!
Mistake to Avoid

Like days of the week, months are not capitalized in Spanish. Of course, if the day of the week or the month comes at the beginning of the sentence, it would be capitalized: *Fui a España en mayo* (I went to Spain in May). *Agosto tiene treinta y un días* (There are thirty-one days in August).

Here are the words for the four seasons in Spanish:

English	Spanish
spring	*la primavera*
summer	*el verano*
autumn	*el otoño*
winter	*el invierno*

What's your favorite season of the year? Why? A little later in this chapter, you'll learn how to talk about weather. This will help you describe your favorite season to your friends!

Gramática — Additional Grammar

Here are three things that are different about dates in Spanish: (1) The definite article (*el*) is used in front of the date; (2) The number always goes in front of the month; (3) *De* goes between the date and month.

What's Today's Date?—*¿Cuál es la fecha de hoy?*

Talking about the date in Spanish is a little bit tricky. To ask What's the date? say *¿Cuál es la fecha?* Then you can answer with *Es el* (It is) plus the date.

Here are some examples:

English	Spanish
It's October 2.	*Es el 2 de octubre.*
It's March 15.	*Es el 15 de marzo.*
It's December 31.	*Es el 31 de diciembre.*

On the first day of the month, instead of saying *uno*, in Spanish you say *primero*, just like how in English you'd say January 1st, not January 1.

English	Spanish
It's May 1st.	*Es el primero de mayo.*
It's July 1st.	*Es el primero de julio.*

When you write the short form of the date in Spanish, the day *still* goes before the month:

English	Spanish
May 30 (5/30)	*mayo 30 (30/5)*
January 20 (1/20)	*enero 20 (20/1)*

Some dates can be really tricky:

English	Spanish
February 3 (2/3)	*febrero 3 (3/2)*
March 2 (3/2)	*marzo 2 (2/3)*

So, you really need to remember that the day goes first in Spanish, otherwise you might get the date completely wrong!

¿Cómo?— Say What?

To ask what day (of the week) it is, say *¿Qué día es hoy?* Then to answer, you just use *Es* plus the day of the week. For example: *Es lunes* (It's Monday); *Es sábado* (It's Saturday).

Weather—*Tiempo*

To talk about the weather, you need to learn a new verb: *hacer*. When followed by weather words related to temperature and the sky, *hacer* means "to be." And the only conjugation you need is *hace* (it is). Here are some important sentences to know:

English	Spanish
How's the weather?	*¿Qué tiempo hace?*
It's bad weather.	*Hace mal tiempo.*
It's cold.	*Hace frío*
It's cool.	*Hace fresco.*
It's hot.	*Hace calor.*
It's nice out.	*Hace buen tiempo.*

As always, there are exceptions. There are times when the verb *hace* doesn't work. In those cases you need to use different verbs. Here are some examples:

It's cloudy.	*Está nublado.*
It's sunny.	*Hay sol o está soleado.*
It's foggy.	*Hay neblina.*

To talk about specific temperatures, you'll also use *hace*:

English	Spanish
It's 10 degrees.	*Hace diez grados.*
It's 5 degrees below zero.	*Hace cinco grados bajo cero.*

For rain, snow, and hail, you need to use *está* (it is):

English	Spanish
It's raining.	*Está lloviendo.*
It's snowing.	*Está nevando.*
It's hailing.	*Está cayendo granizo.*

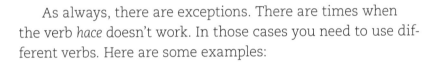

Consejo
IMPORTANT TIP

For temperatures, most countries use Celsius, which can be confusing if you're not used to it. To convert from Fahrenheit to Celsius, take the Fahrenheit temperature, subtract 30, and divide by 2. This will give you an approximate Celsius temperature. For example, 70°F - 30 = 40 ÷ 2 = 20°C. To convert from Celsius to Fahrenheit, it's just the opposite: multiply by 2 and add 30: 10°C × 2 = 20 + 30 = 50°F.

And finally, when you want to say that there is a very severe weather condition like a blizzard, you use *hay* (there is) plus the word:

English	Spanish
blizzard	*una ventisca*
drought	*una sequía*
flood	*una inundación*
hurricane	*un huracán*
tornado	*un tornado*

Holidays—*Días festivos*

Everybody likes to celebrate, but holidays are not the same in every country. Here are some holidays that are celebrated in the United States as well as in many Spanish-speaking countries:

English	Spanish
Christmas	*la Navidad*
Christmas Eve	*la Nochebuena*
Easter	*la Pascua*
Father's Day	*el Día del Padre*
Mother's Day	*el Día de la Madre*
New Year's	*el Año Nuevo*
New Year's Eve	*la Nochevieja*
Valentine's Day	*el Día de San Valentín*

Here are some dates that are special to Spanish speakers.

- **January 6—*Día de los Reyes Magos*:** The celebration of Three Kings Day, also know as *Epifanía* (Epiphany), is important in Catholic countries such as Spain and Latin America. This is often another day for kids to get presents, just like on Christmas.

Diversión—Fun Stuff

Make a calendar using all of your new vocabulary, either with a pen and paper or on the computer. Make a page for each month and label the months and days of the week in Spanish, then add all of the holidays celebrated in Spanish-speaking countries as well as in your own. And don't forget birthdays!

- **May 5—*Cinco de Mayo*:** *Cinco de Mayo*, which of course means May 5th, is a celebration of Mexico's defeat of the French in 1862. It is celebrated in parts of Mexico as well as cities in the United States with large Mexican populations.
- **November 1—*Día de los Muertos*:** *Día de los Muertos*, or Day of the Dead, is a Mexican celebration in honor of friends and loved ones who have died.
- **Holy Week—*Semana Santa*:** *Semana Santa* is an 8-day celebration, from Palm Sunday to Easter Monday, in many Catholic countries, including Spain, and Latin America.

Birthdays—*Cumpleaños*

For many people, birthdays are the most special days of all! Here are some useful phrases for talking about your own birthday, as well as those of your friends and family.

English	Spanish
birthday	*el cumpleaños*
birthday cake	*una torta de cumpleaños*
birthday card	*una tarjeta de cumpleaños*
birthday party	*una fiesta de cumpleaños*
birthday present	*un regalo de cumpleaños*
Happy birthday!	*¡Feliz cumpleaños!*

Consejo
IMPORTANT TIP

In the United States, a girl's "sweet 16th" birthday is considered the most special. But even the fanciest sweet 16 party is nowhere near as elaborate as *el quinceañero*.

In Hispanic countries, a girl's 15th birthday—*la quinceañera*—is the most special. The closest equivalent in the United States is the now old-fashioned coming-out party. In Mexico and other Hispanic countries, 15 is seen as the age when a girl turns into a woman, and this is commemorated with a huge party, with many similarities to a wedding in

the United States, with a church ceremony, a fancy white or light pink dress and matching bouquet, a "court" with *damas* (maids of honor) and *chambelanes* (gentlemen), party favors, and a banquet. I bet you don't know that the party itself has a name and it is called *el quinceañero*. The girl turning 15 is called *la quinceañera*.

To ask how old someone is, say *¿Cuántos años tienes?*

And then to answer, you need to use *tengo*, from the verb *tener* (which normally means "to have") plus the number and then the word *años* (years).

English	Spanish
I'm six years old.	*Tengo seis años.*
I'm ten years old.	*Tengo diez años.*

Nice Party

Find your way from *el principio* (the start) to *el fin* (the end). Circle the number of *regalos de cumpleaños* you travel through.

UNO
DOS
TRES

Have a short conversation with a friend about ages. Here's a sample conversation:

ANA: *Hola, Carlos.*
CARLOS: *Buenos días.*

ANA: *¿Cuántos años tienes?*
CARLOS: *Tengo nueve años.*

ANA: *¡Yo también!*
CARLOS: *¡Qué interesante!*

ANA: *¡Hasta Luego!*
CARLOS: *¡Adios, Ana!*

Now write your own conversation in the blank spaces provided and practice it with a friend:

SPEAKER 1: _____

SPEAKER 2: _____

SPEAKER 1: _____

SPEAKER 2: _____

SPEAKER 1: _____

SPEAKER 2: _____

SPEAKER 1: _____

SPEAKER 2: _____

Birthdays are great! Everyone has one, and it's a great opportunity to throw a party, eat cake, and open presents! You probably know exactly when your own birthday is, but do you know the birthdays of your friends and family members? Fill in the blanks below to help yourself remember these important days. Here's the trick: The months are in Spanish!

Month in Spanish	Friend or Family Member	Birth Date
enero		
febrero		
marzo		
abril		
mayo		
junio		
julio		
agosto		
septiembre		
octubre		
noviembre		
diciembre		

For extra fun, write a short sentence about your own birthday! Find a calendar of the current year and look up what day of the week your birthday falls on. Check out the example below, and then write your own birthday sentence.

My birthday is Tuesday, April 23.   *Mi cumpleaños es el martes, el 23 de abril.*

CHAPTER 8

Food and Drink
Comida y bebida

¿Cómo?— Say What?

Be careful with the word *sopa*. It looks and sounds a lot like "soap," but it really means "soup." The last thing you want to do is order soap when you're at a restaurant!

Meals and Courses—*Comidas y platos*

Eating new foods is one of the best things about traveling. If you go to Spain, Mexico, or another Spanish-speaking country, you'll definitely want to know how to talk about food. Here are some useful words to know:

English	Spanish
meal	*la comida*
breakfast	*el desayuno*
lunch	*el almuerzo*
dinner	*la cena*
appetizer	*el aperitivo*
soup	*la sopa*
sandwich	*el bocadillo, el sándwich*
main course	*el plato principal*
salad	*la ensalada*
dessert	*el postre*

Here is some general food vocabulary that you might find helpful:

English	Spanish
bread	*el pan*
French fries	*las papas fritas*
jam	*la mermelada*
mayonnaise	*la mayonesa*
mustard	*la mostaza*
oil	*el aceite*
omelet	*la tortilla* (in Spain)
pepper	*la pimienta*
rice	*el arroz*
salt	*la sal*
sugar	*el azúcar*
toast	*el pan tostado*

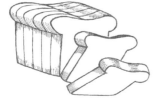

And here are some useful verbs related to eating and drinking.

English	Spanish
to be hungry	*tener hambre*
to eat	*comer*
to be thirsty	*tener sed*
to drink	*beber*

Gramática — Additional Grammar

The Spanish verb *tomar* is often used with food and drink. It means "to take," but you can use it to mean "eat" or "drink."

Fruit and Vegetables—*Frutas y vegetales*

Fruit and vegetables are good for you, but they taste good too! Here are the Spanish words for some delicious fruits:

English	Spanish
apple	*una manzana*
apricot	*un albaricoque*
banana	*un plátano, una banana*
blackberry	*una zarzamora*
blueberry, cranberry	*un arándano*
cherry	*una cereza*
grape	*una uva*

English	Spanish
grapefruit	*una toronja, un pomelo*
lemon	*un limón*
lime	*una lima*
orange	*una naranja*
peach	*un melocotón*
pear	*una pera*
plum	*una ciruela*
raspberry	*una frambuesa*
strawberry	*una fresa*

Don't forget the vegetables!

English	Spanish
artichoke	*la alcachofa*
asparagus	*los espárragos*
beans	*las judías*
carrot	*la zanahoria*
celery	*el apio*
corn	*la mazorca, el maíz*
cucumber	*el pepino*
eggplant	*la berenjena*
garlic	*el ajo*
lettuce	*la lechuga*
mushroom	*el champiñón*
olives	*las aceitunas*
onion	*la cebolla*
peas	*los guisantes*
potato	*la papa, la patata*
radish	*el rábano*
spinach	*las espinacas*
tomato	*el tomate*

For a fun way to learn all the names of the different vegetables in Spanish, pretend you're making a big pot of soup.

Diversión—Fun Stuff

What are your favorite fruits and vegetables? Draw a garden with all of your favorites, and label them in Spanish. If you want to, you can use color, too. Use crayons or markers to draw the garden and then label the different fruits and vegetables with their names and colors. For example, for red strawberries, just write *fresas rojas*.

What kind of soup would you like to make? What ingredients would you include? Fill in the following blank spaces with some of the veggies you'd like to put in your soup.

_____

_____

_____

_____

_____

Diversión_Fun Stuff

Draw a big picture of a pizza and then add a whole bunch of vegetable toppings. Don't forget to label all the veggies in Spanish! Some favorite combinations are spinach and mushroom, peppers and onions, or garlic and tomato. What are your favorites?

Meat and Dairy—*Carne y productos lácteos*

Here are some different kinds of meat and seafood. You'll want to know how to say all of these words in Spanish so you know what you're ordering when you go out to eat at a restaurant in a Spanish-speaking country.

English	Spanish
anchovy	*la anchoa*
beef	*la carne de res*
chicken	*el pollo*
fish	*el pescado*
ham	*el jamón*
lamb	*el cordero*
pork	*el cerdo*
rabbit	*el conejo*
roast beef	*el rosbif*
sausage	*la salchicha*
seafood	*el marisco*
steak	*el bistec*
turkey	*el pavo*
veal	*la ternera*

Consejo
IMPORTANT TIP

Do you remember learning that "fish" is *un pez* in the section on pets in Chapter 5? Well, *pez* is the word for a live fish, but when you talk about a fish that you're going to eat, it's called *pescado*.

LAS PAPAS FRITAS

LA SOPA

EL BOCADILLO

Let's Eat Lunch!

Find the picture suggested by each numbered clue and write the Spanish word into the puzzle grid. We left U-N-A P-I-Z-Z-A to help you out!

EL PAN

LA LECHE

LA FRESA

ACROSS

2 Slices of bread with a filling

5 _____ and crackers

6 Comes hot in a bowl or a cup

8 Autumn fruit of red or green

9 Drink made by a cow

12 Crispy hot potato strips

14 Summer fruit with many seeds

15 Comes in a loaf

16 You pour milk into this

DOWN

1 Summer citrus drink

3 Fruit in a bunch

4 Fruit served in a shortcake

6 Meat served on a bun with ketchup

7 Fruit with a small top and big bottom

10 Fruit with a long, yellow peel

11 Mix of green leaves and veggies

12 Sweet, baked treat eaten with milk

13 Crisp veggie stalk with a leafy top

LA SANDÍA

EL APIO

LAS UVAS

LA ENSALADA

EL PLÁTANO

LA HAMBURGUESA

LA LIMONADA

LA PERA

LA MANZANA

EL HELADO

EL HUEVO

LA GALLETA

EL VASO

EL QUESO

Here are some dairy products:

English	Spanish
butter	*la mantequilla*
buttermilk	*el suero de leche*
cheese	*el queso*
cream	*la crema*
cottage cheese	*el requesón*
ice cream	*el helado*
milk	*la leche*
yogurt	*el yogur*

Drinks—*Bebidas*

Now you just need a drink to go with all that great food! Here are some delicious drinks you might enjoy:

English	Spanish
hot chocolate	*el chocolate*
iced tea	*el té helado*
juice	*el jugo, el zumo*
lemonade	*la limonada*
milk	*la leche*
milkshake	*el batido*
orange juice	*el jugo, el zumo de naranja*
smoothie	*el licuado (de frutas)*
soda/pop	*el refresco*
tea	*el té*
water	*el agua*

Your parents might have one of these drinks:

English	Spanish
beer	*la cerveza*
coffee	*el café*
espresso	*el café exprés*
wine	*el vino*

Dessert—*Postres*

If you still have room after all of that great food, you can have some dessert. Here are some yummy choices:

English	Spanish
cake	*el pastel, la torta*
candy	*el dulce, las golosinas*
chocolate	*el chocolate*
cookie	*la galleta*
custard	*las natillas, el flan*
donut	*la rosquilla, la dónut*
fritter	*el buñuelo*
fruit	*la fruta*
ice cream	*el helado*
muffin	*la magdalena*
pie	*la tarta, el pastel*
rice pudding	*el arroz con leche*
vanilla	*la vainilla*

el helado

Consejo
IMPORTANT TIP

Ice is *el hielo* in Spanish. To ask for ice in your drink, say *con hielo*. If you don't want ice, say *sin hielo*. *Con* means "with" and *sin* means "without."

Here are some different kinds of nuts you might find in your dessert:

English	Spanish
almonds	*las almendras*
cashews	*los anacardos*
peanuts	*los cacahuetes*
pistachios	*los pistachos*
walnuts	*las nueces*

Now it's time to practice all the food words you've learned. Create a menu with what you'd like to eat for breakfast, lunch, and dinner for one day—in Spanish, of course! Don't forget to include healthy foods like fruits and vegetables. Fill in the blanks to make your menu:

El desayuno (breakfast)

_____

_____

_____

El almuerzo (lunch)

_____

_____

_____

La cena (dinner)

_____

_____

_____

El postre (dessert)

_____

Hidden Foods

Can you find the five Spanish food words hidden in the following sentences? Look for words in the word list, but be careful—some words are not used!

WORD LIST
la fruta
la tarta
flan
la patata
el apio
la carne
la sal
el pepino
el pan

1. Food fight! Splat art! Annoy mom!
2. In a tunnel, a car never goes fast.
3. A morsel, Pa. Not a lot!
4. I eat food of land and sea.
5. I will fill a salad bowl.

Gramática — Additional Grammar

Vegetarian is an adjective and just like all adjectives, it will change to agree with the gender and number of the noun it modifies. So if you're a girl, you'll say *Soy vegetariana*. If you're talking about more than one person, you would say *Somos vegetarianos* (We are vegetarians).

¿Cómo?— Say What?

¡Buen provecho! is a useful expression and is used a lot more than "enjoy your meal" is in English. It's a polite expression used just before everyone starts to eat.

At the Restaurant—*En el restaurante*

When you go to a restaurant, you need to know more than just the names for food. You also need to be able to order what you want and maybe even explain that you can't eat certain things. This section will serve as your restaurant survival guide!

To order, you can either say *Me gustaría* or *Quisiera*. Both of these mean "I would like" and they are very polite. If you want to ask how much something costs, say *¿Cuánto cuesta...?*

If you need to explain what you can and can't eat before you order, you might find these phrases helpful:

English	Spanish
I can't eat...	*No puedo comer...*
I don't like...	*No me gusta...*
I'm allergic to...	*Tengo alergia a...*
I'm a vegetarian.	*Soy vegetariano.*

If you order meat, you might need to specify how you'd like it cooked.

English	Spanish
rare	*poco cocida*
medium	*medio cocida*
well done	*muy bien cocida*

Here are some other useful restaurant phrases:

English	Spanish
menu	*la carta*
check/bill	*la cuenta*
tip	*la propina*
tip included	*servicio incluido*

CHAPTER 9

Who are you?
¿Quién eres?

Where Do You Live?—*¿Dónde vives?*

When you travel or meet people, one of the first things you will probably talk about is where you live.

To ask where someone lives, say *¿Dónde vives?*

The answer begins with *Vivo en* (I live in), followed by a city, state, province, or country.

English	Spanish
Where do you live?	*¿Dónde vives?*
I live in Detroit.	*Vivo en Detroit.*
I live in California.	*Vivo en California.*
I live in Canada.	*Vivo en Canadá.*
I live near Los Angeles.	*Vivo cerca de Los Angeles.*
I live near Chicago.	*Vivo cerca de Chicago.*

To ask where someone is from (which might not be the same as where he or she lives now), ask *¿De dónde eres?* And then you can answer *Soy de* (I'm from) or *Nací en* (I was born in).

English	Spanish
Where are you from?	*¿De dónde eres?*
I'm from Houston.	*Soy de Houston.*
I'm from Ontario.	*Soy de Ontario.*
I was born in Portland.	*Nací en Portland.*
I was born in New York.	*Nací en Nueva York.*

You might also want to say that you used to live somewhere:

English	Spanish
I used to live in San Francisco.	*Antes viví en San Francisco.*
I used to live in Florida.	*Antes viví en Florida.*

¿Cómo?— Say What?

If you live in a small town that people in other countries have never heard of, you might like to say *Vivo cerca de* (I live near) and then the nearest city.

And finally, if you want to keep in touch with someone, you'll need to give them your address or phone number.

English	Spanish
My address is	*Mi dirección es*
My email address is	*Mi dirección electrónica es*
My phone number is	*Mi número de teléfono es*

Countries—*Países*

Knowing the Spanish words for different countries will be useful in many ways: for talking about where you are from and where you are traveling to, as well as understanding where the people you meet are from.

Many places have the same name in Spanish and English:

- Argentina
- Asia
- Australia
- Chile
- China
- Colombia
- Costa Rica
- Ecuador
- India
- Puerto Rico
- Portugal

Here are a couple of sample sentences to guide you:

English	Spanish
I want to go to Australia.	*Quiero ir a Australia.*
I went to Costa Rica last year.	*Fui a Costa Rica el año pasado.*

Consejo
IMPORTANT TIP

To say "My email address is *myname@network.com*," for example, you would say *Mi dirección electrónica es myname arroba network punto com.*

Gramática —
Additional Grammar

Like all other vocabulary, the Spanish words for countries have gender. If the word ends in *a,* it's feminine: la Colombia, la Francia. Otherwise, it's masculine: el Portugal, el México. Now, you will not use pronouns when talking about the country by itself. So to say "France is a very nice country," you would omit the pronoun and just say *Francia es un país muy bello.* You would use the pronouns when you are talking about certain characteristics of the country; for example, to say "A common food in ancient Mexico was corn," you would say *El maíz era una comida común en el México antiguo.*

But for others, the words are different in Spanish and English.

English	Spanish	English	Spanish
Africa	*África*	Italy	*Italia*
Brazil	*Brasil*	Japan	*Japón*
Canada	*Canadá*	Mexico	*México*
Egypt	*Egipto*	Poland	*Polonia*
England	*Inglaterra*	Russia	*Rusia*
Europe	*Europa*	Spain	*España*
France	*Francia*	Switzerland	*Suiza*
Germany	*Alemania*	United States	*Estados Unidos*

Nationality—*Nacionalidad*

Another way to talk about where you're from is to talk about your nationality. For example, if you are from America, you are American. Here are some other nationalities in the world:

English	Spanish
African	*africano*
American (United States)	*estadounidense*
American (North or South)	*americano*
Argentine	*argentino*
Asian	*asiático*
Australian	*australiano*
Brazilian	*brasileño*
Canadian	*canadiense*
Chilean	*chileno*
Chinese	*chino*
Colombian	*colombiano*
Costa Rican	*costarricense*
Ecuadoran	*ecuatoriano*
Egyptian	*egipcio*

Consejo
IMPORTANT TIP

Just as United States of America has the abbreviation U.S.A., *los Estados Unidos* is abbreviated to *los EE.UU.*

English	Spanish
English	*inglés*
European	*europeo*
French	*francés*
German	*alemán*
Indian	*indio*
Italian	*italiano*
Japanese	*japonés*
Mexican	*mexicano*
Polish	*polaco*
Portuguese	*portugués*
Puerto Rican	*puertorriqueño*
Russian	*ruso*
Spanish	*español*
Swiss	*suizo*

English	Spanish
I am American.	*Soy estadounidense.*
My mom is a Spaniard.	*Mi madre es española.*

Languages—*Idiomas*

There are hundreds of languages in the world. Here are the Spanish names for the ones you might need to talk about.

English	Spanish
Arabic	*el árabe*
Catalan	*el catalán*
Chinese	*el chino*
Dutch	*el neerlandés*
English	*el inglés*
French	*el francés*
German	*el alemán*

¡CUIDADO!
Mistake to Avoid

In Spanish, all languages are masculine and are not capitalized. The same is true for nationalities. For example: the Spanish language would be *el idioma español*, and He is a Spaniard would be *Él es español.*

Italian	el italiano
Japonese	el japonés
Korean	el coreano
Persian	el persa
Polish	el polaco
Portuguese	el portugués
Russian	el ruso
Spanish	el español
Vietnamese	el vietnamita

¿Cómo?— Say What?

The Spanish spoken in Spain is known as Castilian Spanish. It is different from the Spanish spoken in Latin America, just as the English spoken in the United States is different from English in England.

English	Spanish
I speak English and Spanish.	*Hablo inglés y español.*
I don't speak German.	*No hablo alemán.*

Do you know anyone who speaks a second language? Perhaps one of your parents learned another language in college, or you have a friend from a different country. For some more writing practice, write down some sentences explaining who of your friends and family speaks another language. Remember that the words for different languages are lowercased when written in Spanish. Here are a couple of examples:

English	Spanish
My mother speaks Italian.	*Mi madre habla italiano.*
My friend speaks French.	*Mi amigo habla francés.*

Now try writing your own sentences in the spaces below:

_____

_____

_____

_____

Tricky Traveler

A silly joke and its answer have been put into a puzzle grid. The grid has been cut into pieces and scattered around the page. Figure out which puzzle piece goes where, and fill the letters into the correct spaces of the empty grid. Use the vocabulary list to help you translate the answer!

Vocabulary List
el ABRIGO = COAT
los BRAZOS = ARMS
CANSADOS = TIRED
el GATO = CAT
MIS = MY
MUY = VERY
los PIES = FEET
SON = ARE
el TREN = TRAIN

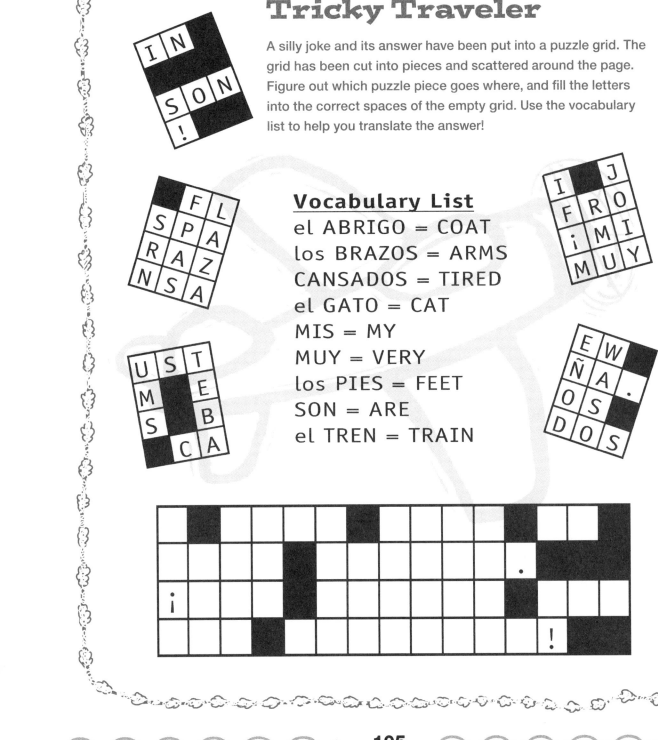

Gramática —
Additional Grammar

To ask someone else about his or her dreams, use *¿Qué quieres _____?* (What do you want) or *¿Dónde quieres _____?* (Where do you want) followed by *ir* (to go), *vivir* (to live), or *ser* (to be). *¿Qué quieres ser?* (What do you want to be?) *¿Dónde quieres vivir?* (Where do you want to live?)

When I Grow Up...—*Cuando sea grande...*

What do you want to be when you grow up? What do you want to do, where do you want to live? This section will help you talk about all of your dreams for the future.

English	Spanish
I want to be...	*Quiero ser...*
I want to be a fireman.	*Quiero ser bombero.*
I want to be a doctor.	*Quiero ser médico.*
I'm going to be...	*Voy a ser...*
I'm going to be an artist.	*Voy a ser artista.*
I'm going to be a teacher.	*Voy a ser profesor.*
I don't want to be...	*No quiero ser...*
I don't want to be a writer.	*No quiero ser escritor.*
I don't want to be a manager.	*No quiero ser gerente.*
I want to live in...	*Quiero vivir en...*
I want to live in Spain.	*Quiero vivir en España.*
I want to live in Buenos Aires.	*Quiero vivir en Buenos Aires.*
I don't want to live in...	*No quiero vivir en...*
I don't want to live in the US.	*No quiero vivir en los EE.UU.*
I don't want to live in Miami.	*No quiero vivir en Miami.*
I dream of...	*Mi sueño es...*
I dream of traveling around Spain.	*Mi sueño es viajar por España.*
I dream of being president.	*Mi sueño es ser presidente.*

Sports—*Deportes*

Well, you've made it through nine chapters, learning the vocabulary you need to talk about what you have to do. Now you can finally learn how to talk about what you do to have fun!

If you like to play sports, here is the Spanish for the most common ones. For all of these, you can say *Me gusta* (I like) or *No me gusta* (I don't like). You can also say *Juego a* (I play) and *Miro* (I watch).

English	Spanish
baseball	*el béisbol*
basketball	*el baloncesto*
football	*el fútbol americano*
golf	*el golf*
hockey	*el hockey*
rugby	*el rugby*
soccer	*el fútbol*
tennis	*el tenis*
volleyball	*el voleibol, el balonvolea*

For example:

English	Spanish
I like baseball.	*Me gusta el béisbol.*
I don't like tennis.	*No me gusta el tenis.*
I play soccer.	*Juego al fútbol.*

For a few sports you can't use *juego* because you don't play them. Instead, you use the verb for "doing" the sport. But you can still use *Me gusta*, *No me gusta*, and *Miro*. Here are some sports that you "use the action verb" instead of "play" as well as examples of *Me gusta* and *Miro*.

English	Spanish
boxing	*el boxeo*
skating	*el patinaje*
skiing	*el esquí*
wrestling	*la lucha*

For example:

English	Spanish
I box.	*Yo boxeo.*
I like skating.	*Me gusta el patinaje.*
I watch wrestling.	*Miro la lucha.*

**¿Cómo?—
Say What?**

There are a few different variations on skiing and skating in both English and Spanish. In Spanish, water-skiing is *el esquí acuático*, while cross-country skiing is *el esquí de fondo*. Ice skating is *el patinaje sobre hielo* and roller skating is *el patinaje sobre ruedas*.

Games—*Juegos*

For games, you can use the same verbs as for sports: *Juego a*, *Me gusta*, and *No me gusta*. Here are some games you might like to play with friends and family:

English	Spanish
board game	*un juego de tablero*
backgammon	*el backgammon*
checkers	*las damas*
chess	*el ajedrez*
Chinese checkers	*las damas chinas*
dominoes	*el dominó*
parcheesi	*el parchís*
card game	*un juego de cartas/de naipes/de barajas*
bridge	*el bridge*
gin rummy	*el gin rummy*
hearts	*los corazones*
poker	*el póquer*
rummy	*el rummy*
solitaire	*el solitario*

un juego de cartas

Here are some sample sentences:

English	Spanish
I play chess.	*Juego al ajedrez.*
I like dominoes.	*Me gusta el dominó.*
I don't like solitaire.	*No me gusta el solitario.*

Consejo
IMPORTANT TIP

In Spanish-speaking countries, there are two different decks of cards. The traditional cards you know and play with in the United States are known in Spanish as *barajas francesas* (French cards) and also there is a special deck of Spanish cards called *naipes españoles* that has different suits and drawings. The four suits in the traditional cards are called *corazones* (hearts), *diamantes* (diamonds), *picas* (spades), and *tréboles* (clubs). You already know all the numbers, but you might need help with the face cards: *as* (ace), *sota* (jack), *reina* (queen), and *rey* (king). And don't forget the joker: *¡el comodín!*

The suits in the Spanish cards are *oros* (gold pieces), *espadas* (swords), *copas* (cups), and *bastos* (clubs). They are very colorful and you can play games you've never even heard of before.

I Win!

Use the decoder to find a Spanish word to answer the riddle. What does this word mean? Add the numbers used in the answer and check the key!

 =A

♥2 =D

♦3 =L

♣1 ♠5   ♥2 ♣1 ♛4 ♣1 ♠5

♛4 =M

—— —— —— —— —— —— —— ——

♠5 =S

KEY: | 20 JUMP ROPE | 21 HOPSCOTCH | 22 CHECKERS |

Here are some other games you might enjoy:

English	Spanish
darts	*los dardos*
pinball machine	*máquina del millón*
ping pong	*el tenis de mesa, el ping-pong*
pool	*el billar americano*
videogame	*un videojuego*

What do you like to play? Make a list of the games you like the most using the blank spaces below.

_____

_____

_____

_____

Now compare the games you like with the games your friends like. To ask a friend what he or she likes, ask, *¿Qué te gusta?*

Activities—*Actividades*

Here are some other kinds of outside activities that you might enjoy with your friends and family:

English	Spanish
biking	*el ciclismo*
fishing	*la pesca*
gardening	*la jardinería*
hiking	*el excursionismo*
hunting	*la caza*
jogging	*el footing*
running	*correr*
sailing	*la navegación a vela*
skateboarding	*el monopatinaje*
swimming	*la natación*

Gramática —
Additional Grammar

Talking about hunting and fishing is different than talking about most activities, which need the verb *Hago* (I do). For hunting and fishing, you use *Voy* (I go) instead: *Voy de caza* (I go hunting) and *Voy de pesca* (I go fishing).

la natación

And some indoor activities:

English	Spanish
collecting	el coleccionismo
cooking	la cocina
jigsaw puzzle	el rompecabezas
juggling	el malabarismo
magic	la magia
reading	la lectura
writing	la escritura

Here are some sample sentences:

English	Spanish
I like cooking.	Me gusta la cocina.
I don't like juggling.	No me gusta el malabarismo.

¿Cómo?—Say What?

What do you like to collect? How about dolls (*muñecas*), stamps (*sellos*), rubber stamps (*estampillas*), coins (*monedas*), comic books (*revistas cómics*), marbles (*canicas*), or toy cars (*coches de juguete*)?

TV and Movies—*Televisión y películas*

Watching movies and television can be fun, and they can also teach you all about people, places, and things. Here are some Spanish words relating to movies:

English	Spanish
movie	una película
movie theater	un cine
action movie	una película de acción
classic movie	una película clásica
comedy	una comedia
documentary	un documental
drama	un drama
horror movie	una película de terror
romance movie	una película romántica
romantic comedy	una comedia romántica

Ask your parents if you can rent a Spanish movie and watch it together. This is a great way to see how much Spanish you've actually learned. When the movie is over, talk about what kind of movie it was, what you liked about it, and what you didn't like about it.

¡CUIDADO!
Mistake to Avoid

Be careful—*programa* ends in *a*, but it's masculine. For example: *Es un nuevo programa* means It's a new program.

Here are some words to use when talking about television:

English	Spanish
television	*la televisión*
cartoon	*unos dibujos animados*
miniseries	*una miniserie*
sitcom	*una comedia de situación*
soap opera	*una telenovela*
TV show	*un programa de televisión*
TV station	*una estación de televisión*
TV network	*una cadena de televisión*

Music and Dance—*Música y baile*

Do you like music? Of course you do! But what kind of music do you like? Here are some words to help you chat about music:

English	Spanish
music	*la música*
blues	*los blues*
classical	*la música clásica*
country music	*la música country*
folk music	*la música folklórica*
heavy metal	*el heavy metal*
jazz	*el jazz*
rap	*el rap*
rock and roll	*el rock and roll*

With music, you can use *Me gusta* and *No me gusta* again. For example:

English	Spanish
I like classical music.	*Me gusta la música clásica.*
I don't like jazz.	*No me gusta el jazz.*

Or maybe you like to play music. Here are some instruments:

la guitarra

English	Spanish
drum	*el tambor*
flute	*la flauta*
guitar	*la guitarra*
piano	*el piano*
saxophone	*el saxofón*
trumpet	*la trompeta*
violin	*el violín*

To play an instrument, use *Toco:*

English	Spanish
I play the violin.	*Toco el violín.*
I play the flute.	*Toco la flauta.*

Do you like to dance? Here are some kinds of dance and some other words to use with them.

English	Spanish
dancing	*el baile*
ballet	*el ballet*
ballroom dancing	*el baile de salón*
hip hop	*el hip hop*
jazz	*el jazz*
modern	*el baile moderno*
tap dance	*el claqué*

Gramática — Additional Grammar

Another verb you can use is *Escucho* (I listen to). *Escucho el rap*—I listen to rap (music). *No escucho el rock and roll*—I don't listen to rock and roll. And if you sing, you need the verb *cantar*. To say "I sing," say *Canto*.

Consejo
IMPORTANT TIP

There are many different types of music and dance from the Spanish-speaking world: *tango* from Argentina, *flamenco* from Spain, *mambo* and *rumba* from Cuba, *merengue* from the Dominican Republic, and *mariachi* from Mexico. Have you heard of any of these?

Arts and Crafts—*Arte y manualidades*

If you're the artistic type, you'll probably find some of this vocabulary helpful.

¿Cómo?— Say What?

Art projects like knitting and needlepoint are done with yarn and string. In Spanish, both of these materials are called *el hilo,* but yarn can also be called *el hilo de lana.* If you need a needle, that's *una aguja.*

English	Spanish
crocheting	*hacer ganchillo*
embroidery	*el bordado*
knitting	*tejer*
macrame	*el macramé*
needlepoint	*el cañamazo*
quilting	*hacer edredones*
sewing	*coser*
weaving	*tejer*
basketry	*la cestería*
collage	*el collage*
drawing	*dibujar*
painting	*pintar*
photography	*la fotografía*
pottery	*la alfarería*
rubber stamps	*las estampillas de goma*
sculpture	*la escultura*
scrapbook	*el álbum de recortes*
woodworking	*la carpintería*

If you could do whatever you wanted every day, would you just play the same game all the time, or would you play soccer on Monday and paint on Tuesday? Use the following spaces to write up your dream schedule—in Spanish, of course!

lunes	*martes*	*miércoles*	*jueves*	*viernes*	*sábado*	*domingo*
___	___	___	___	___	___	___
___	___	___	___	___	___	___
___	___	___	___	___	___	___
___	___	___	___	___	___	___

Nifty Knitter

While this girl practices her *labor de punto* (knitting), you can match the six words that are sounded out to the correct words in the word list. Then look for these items hidden in the picture!

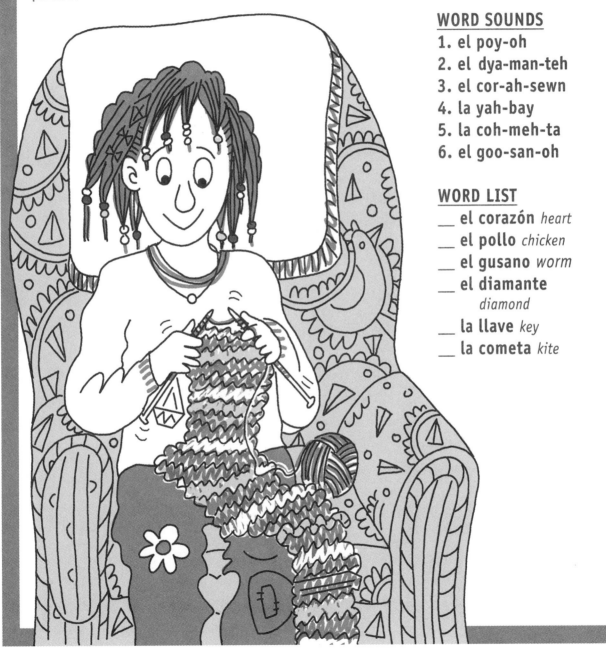

WORD SOUNDS
1. el poy-oh
2. el dya-man-teh
3. el cor-ah-sewn
4. la yah-bay
5. la coh-meh-ta
6. el goo-san-oh

WORD LIST
__ **el corazón** *heart*
__ **el pollo** *chicken*
__ **el gusano** *worm*
__ **el diamante**
     diamond
__ **la llave** *key*
__ **la cometa** *kite*

English-Spanish Glossary

English	Spanish	English	Spanish
accent	un acento	artist	un/una artista
action movie	una película de acción	Asian	asiático
actor/actress	un actor, una actriz	asparagus	los espárragos
adding machine	una sumadora	athletic	atlético
Africa	África	attic	el desván
African	africano	August	agosto
airport	el aeropuerto	aunt	la tía
alarm clock	un despertador	Australian	australiano
almonds	las almendras	autumn	el otoño
American (North + South)	americano	baby	un bebé
		back	la espalda
American (United States)	estadounidense	backgammon	el backgammon
		backpack	una mochila
anchovy	la anchoa	baggage	el equipaje
and	y	baggage claim	el reclamo de equipaje
And you?	¿Y tú?	baker	un panadero, una panadera
angry	enojado	bakery	la panadería
ankle	el tobillo	balcony	el balcón
annoyed	enfadado	ballet	el ballet
ant	una hormiga	ballroom dancing	el baile de salón
appetizer	el aperitivo	banana	un plátano
apple	una manzana	bank	el banco
apricot	un albaricoque	barber	la barbería
April	abril	baseball	el béisbol
Arabic	el árabe	basement	el sótano
arch	un arco	basketball	el baloncesto
Argentine	argentino	basketry	la cestería
arm	el brazo	bathing suit	un traje de baño
Arrivals	Llegadas	bathroom	el baño
art	el arte	bathtub	una bañera, un baño
artichoke	la alcachofa	beans	las judías

English	Spanish
beauty shop	la peluquería
bed	una cama
bedroom	el dormitorio
beef	la carne de res
beer	la cerveza
belt	un cinturón
bicycle	la bicicleta
biking	el ciclismo
bikini	un biquini
biology	la biología
bird	un pájaro
birthday	el cumpleaños
birthday cake	una torta, un pastel de cumpleaños
birthday card	una tarjeta de cumpleaños
birthday party	una fiesta de cumpleaños
birthday present	un regalo de cumpleaños
black	negro
black hair	el cabello o pelo negro
blackberry	una zarzamora
blizzard	una ventisca
blond hair	el cabello o pelo rubio
blouse	una blusa
blue	azul
blueberry	un arándano
blues	los blues
board game	un juego de tablero
boarding pass	la tarjeta de embarque
boat	el barco
book	un libro
bookshelf	una estantería
boots	unas botas
bored	aburrido
boring	aburrido
bottle	una botella
bowl	un bol
box	una caja
boxer shorts	unos calzones
boxing	el boxeo
boy	un niño, un chico
boyfriend	un novio

English	Spanish
bra	un sostén
bracelet	un brazalete
brave	valiente
Brazil	Brasil
Brazilian	brasileño
bread	el pan
breakfast	el desayuno
bridge	el bridge
briefcase	un maletín
brother	el hermano
brown	marrón
brown hair	el cabello, pelo marrón
bus	el autobús
butcher	la carnicería
butter	la mantequilla
buttermilk	el suero de leche
bye	chao
bye-bye	adiosito
cake	la torta, el pastel
calculator	una calculadora
can	una lata
Canada	Canadá
Canadian	canadiense
candy	el dulce, las golosinas
candy store	la confitería
car	el coche, el auto
card game	un juego de cartas
carpenter	un carpintero, una carpintera
carpet	una moqueta
carrot	la zanahoria
carry-on luggage	el equipaje de mano
cartoon	unos dibujos animados
cashews	los anacardos
cashier	un cajero, una cajera
cat	un gato, una gata
Catalan	el catalán
Catch you later!	¡Nos vemos!
CD-ROM	un CD-ROM
ceiling	el techo
celery	el apio
chair	una silla

English	Spanish	English	Spanish
chalk	una tiza	cookie sheet	una bandeja de horno
chalkboard	una pizarra	cooking	la cocina
check, bill	la cuenta	copy machine	una copiadora
checked luggage	el equipaje registrado	corn	la mazorca
checkers	las damas	Costa Rican	costarricense
check-in desk	el mostrador de registro	cottage cheese	el requesón
cheek	la mejilla	couch	un canapé
cheese	el queso	country music	la música country
chemistry	la química	cousin	el primo, la prima
cherry	una cereza	crayons	lápices de colores
chess	el ajedrez	cream	la crema
chest	el pecho	crescent	una media luna
chicken	el pollo	crocheting	hacer ganchillo
Chilean	chileno	cube	un cubo
Chinese	el chino	cucumber	el pepino
Chinese checkers	las damas chinas	cup	una taza
chocolate	el chocolate	curly hair	el cabello, pelo rizado
Christmas	la Navidad	currency exchange	el cambio de moneda
Christmas Eve	la Nochebuena	curtain	una cortina
circle	un círculo	curve	una curva
civics	la educación cívica	custard	las natillas, el flan
class	una clase	customs	la aduana
classic movie	una película clásica	cylinder	un cilindro
classical music	la música clásica	dancing	el baile
classroom	una aula	dark hair	el cabello, pelo oscuro
closet	un clóset, un armario empotrado	dark purple	violeta oscuro
		dark red	rojo oscuro
clothesline	la cuerda para la ropa	darts	los dardos
clothing store	la ropería	database	una base de datos
coat	un abrigo	daughter	la hija
coffee	el café	December	diciembre
cold	frío	den	el salón
collage	el collage	dentist	el/la dentista
collecting	el coleccionismo	department store	los grandes almacenes, las tiendas por departamentos
college	una universidad		
Colombian	colombiano	Departures	Salidas
comedy	una comedia	depressed	deprimido
computer	una computadora	desk	un escritorio
cone	un cono	dessert	el postre
cook	un cocinero, una cocinera	diamond	un diamante
cookie	la galleta	dictionary	un diccionario

English	Spanish	English	Spanish
dining room	el comedor	email	el correo electrónico
dinner	la cena	email address	la dirección electrónica
dishwasher	una lavavajillas	embarrassed	avergonzado
disk drive	una unidad de disco	embroidery	el bordado
dizzy	mareado	employee	un empleado, una empleada
doctor	un doctor, una doctora	enemy	un enemigo, una enemiga
documentary	un documental	engineer	un ingeniero, una ingeniera
dog	un perro, una perra	England	Inglaterra
doghouse	la caseta del perro	English	el inglés
dominoes	el dominó	eraser	un borrador
don't mention it	no hay de qué	espresso	el café exprés
donut	la rosquilla, la dónut	Europe	Europa
door	una puerta	European	europeo
down	abajo	excited	entusiasmado
Dr.	Doctor, Dr.	excuse me	con permiso
drama	un drama	eye	el ojo
drawing	el dibujo	eye doctor	el optometrista
dress	un vestido	face	la cara
dresser	un tocador	far	lejos
driver	un conductor	fat	gordo
driveway	la entrada	Father's Day	el Día del Padre
drought	una sequía	fax machine	una máquina de fax
drum	el tambor	fear	miedo
dry cleaner	la tintorería	February	febrero
dryer	una secadora	fence	la valla
Dutch	el neerlandés	ferret	un hurón
ear	la oreja	ferry	el transbordador
earrings	unos aretes	fifteen	quince
east	este	fifty	cincuenta
Easter	la Pascua	file	un fichero
economy (coach) class	la clase económica	file folder	una carpeta
Ecuadoran	ecuatoriano	filing cabinet	un fichero
eggplant	la berenjena	finger	el dedo
Egypt	Egipto	fingernail	la uña
Egyptian	egipcio	fireman	un bombero, una bombera
eight	ocho	first class	la primera clase
eighteen	dieciocho	fish	un pez
eighty	ochenta	fish (to eat)	el pescado
elbow	el codo	fishing	la pesca
electrician	un/una electricista	five	cinco
eleven	once	flight	un vuelo

English	Spanish	English	Spanish
flight attendant	un/una auxiliar de vuelo	gloves	unos guantes
flood	una inundación	glue	la cola
floor	el suelo	golf	el golf
flower	la flor	Good afternoon	Buenas tardes
flute	la flauta	Good evening	Buenas noches
folk music	la música folklórica	Good night	Buenas noches
foot	el pie	Goodbye	Adiós
football	el fútbol americano	good-looking	guapo, guapa
forgive me	perdóneme, discúlpeme	granddaughter	la nieta
fork	un tenedor	grandfather	el abuelo
forty	cuarenta	grandmother	la abuela
four	cuatro	grandson	el nieto
fourteen	catorce	grape	una uva
France	Francia	grapefruit	una toronja
French	el francés	gray	gris
French fries	las papas fritas	green	verde
Friday	viernes	grocery store	la tienda de comestibles
friend	un amigo	guinea pig	un cobayo
friendly	amistoso	guitar	la guitarra
fritter	el buñuelo	gym, physical education	la educación física
frog	una rana	hair	el cabello, el pelo
fruit	la fruta	hall	el pasillo
fruit stand	la frutería	ham	el jamón
frying pan	una sartén	hammock	la hamaca
funny	divertido	hamster	un hámster
garage	el garaje	hand	la mano
garden	el jardín	happy	feliz, alegre
gardening	la jardinería	Happy birthday!	¡Feliz cumpleaños!
garlic	el ajo	hard drive	un disco duro
gate	la verja	hardware	el hardware
gate (at airport)	una puerta	hardware store	la ferretería
geography	la geografía	hat	un sombrero
gerbil	un gerbo	Have a nice day	Que tenga(s) un buen día
German	el alemán	He is...	Él es...
Germany	Alemania	head	la cabeza
gin rummy	el gin rummy	heart	un corazón
girl	una niña, una chica, una muchacha	hearts	los corazones
		heavy metal	el heavy metal
girlfriend	una novia	helicopter	el helicóptero
glass	un vaso	Hello	Hola
glasses	unas gafas	Her name is...	Ella se llama...

English	Spanish
hermit crab	un cangrejo ermitaño
hexagon	un hexágono
Hi	Hola
high school	un colegio
high-heeled shoes	unos zapatos de tacones altos
highlighter	un marcador
hiking	el excursionismo
hip hop	el hip hop
His name is...	Él se llama...
history	la historia
hockey	el hockey
home economics	la ciencia del hogar
homework	la tarea
horror movie	una película de terror
horse	un caballo
hose	la manga
hospital	el hospital
hot	calor
hot chocolate	el chocolate caliente
hotel	el hotel
how	cómo
How are you?	¿Cómo está(s)?
How do you say _____ in Spanish?	¿Cómo se dice _____ en español?
How do you spell _____?	¿Cómo se escribe _____?
how much	cúanto
How's it going?	¿Qué tal?
huge	enorme
hungry	hambre
hunting	la caza
hurricane	un huracán
husband	el esposo
I can't eat...	No puedo comer...
I don't know	No sé
I don't like...	No me gusta...
I have a question	Tengo una pregunta
I live in	Vivo en
I live near	Vivo cerca de
I thank you	Le doy gracias
I want	Quiero, Deseo
I was born in	Nací en

English	Spanish
I would like	Quisiera
ice cream	el helado
iced tea	el té helado
I'm a vegetarian	Soy vegetariano, soy vegetariana
I'm allergic to...	Tengo alergia a...
I'm from	Soy de
I'm going...	Yo voy...
I'm good	(Estoy) bien
I'm great	(Estoy) muy bien
I'm sorry	Lo siento
I'm very sorry	Lo siento mucho
immigration	la inmigración
impatient	impaciente
in back of	detrás de
in front of	enfrente de
index card	una ficha
Indian	indio
interesting	interesante
Internet	el Internet
Internet browser	un motor de búsqueda
Internet café	un cibercafé
Italian	el italiano
Italy	Italia
itchy	comezón
It's bad weather	Hace mal tiempo
It's cloudy	Está nublado
It's cold	Hace frío
It's cool	Hace fresco, Está fresco
It's foggy	Hay neblina
It's hot	Hace calor
It's nice out	Hace buen tiempo
It's nice to meet you	Mucho gusto
It's sunny	Hay sol, está soleado
It's windy	Hace viento
It is...	Está...
jacket	una chaqueta
jam	la mermelada
January	enero
Japan	Japón
Japanese	el japonés

English-Spanish Glossary

English	Spanish	English	Spanish
jar	un pote	macrame	el macramé
jazz dance	el jazz-ballet	magic	la magia
jazz music	el jazz	maid	una criada
jealous	celoso	mail	el correo
jet ski	la moto acuática	mail carrier	un cartero, una cartera
jigsaw puzzle	el rompecabezas	mailbox	el buzón
jogging	el footing	main course	el plato principal
Judaism	el judaísmo	man	un hombre
juggling	el malabarismo	manager	un/una gerente
juice	el jugo, el zumo	map	un mapa
July	julio	March	marzo
June	junio	market	el mercado
keyboard	un teclado	math	las matemáticas
kind	amable	May	mayo
kitchen	la cocina	May I... ?	¿Puedo... ?
knee	la rodilla	mayonnaise	la mayonesa
knife	un cuchillo	Me too	Yo también
knitting	tejer	meal	la comida
Korean	el coreano	mean	mezquino
lamb	el cordero	mechanic	un mecánico, una mecánica
lamp	una lámpara	medium	mediano
laptop (computer)	una computadora portátil	menu	la carta
large	grande	Mexican	mexicano
Latin	el latín	Mexico	México
laundromat	la lavandería	milk	la leche
lawyer	un abogado, una abogada	milkshake	el batido
layover	una escala	miniseries	una miniserie
lazy	perezoso	mirror	un espejo
left	a la izquierda	Miss	Señorita
leg	la pierna	mittens	unos mitones
lemon	un limón	modern dance	el baile moderno
lemonade	la limonada	Monday	lunes
lettuce	la lechuga	monitor	un monitor
light blue	azul claro	Mother's Day	el Día de la Madre
light green	verde claro	motorbike	la moto
lime	una lima	motorboat	la lancha a motor
line	una línea	motorcycle	la motocicleta
lip	el labio	mouse	un ratón
long	largo	mouth	la boca
long hair	el cabello o pelo largo	movie	una película
lunch	el almuerzo	movie theater	el cine

English	Spanish
Mr.	Señor
Mrs.	Señora
muffin	la magdalena
museum	el museo
mushroom	el champiñón
music	la música
mustard	la mostaza
My address is	Mi dirección es
my best friend	mi mejor amigo
My email address is	Mi dirección electrónica es
My name is...	Me llamo...
My phone number is	Mi número de teléfono es
napkin	una servilleta
narrow	estrecho
near	cerca
neck	el cuello
necklace	un collar
needlepoint	el cañamazo
neighbor	un vecino, una vecina
nephew	el sobrino
nervous	inquieto, nervioso
New Year's	el Año Nuevo
New Year's Eve	la Nochevieja
next to	junto a
nice	simpático
niece	la sobrina
nightgown	un camisón
nine	nueve
nineteen	diecinueve
ninety	noventa
no	no
north	norte
nose	la nariz
notebook	un cuaderno
Nothing (is new)	Nada, sin novedad
Nothing much	Nada de particular
November	noviembre
nurse	un enfermero, una enfermera
octagon	un octágono
October	octubre
offended	ofendido

English	Spanish
office	una oficina
oil	el aceite
OK	de acuerdo
old	viejo
olive	la aceituna
omelet	la tortilla (in Spain)
one	uno, una
one hundred	cien
one million	millón
one thousand	mil
one-way ticket	un billete sencillo
onion	la cebolla
or	o
orange (color)	anaranjado
orange (fruit)	una naranja
orange juice	el jugo, el zumo de naranja
outgoing	abierto
oval	un óvalo
oven	un horno
overseas	al extranjero
painting	la pintura
pajamas	un pijama
panties	unas bragas
pants	unos pantalones
paper	el papel
paper clip	un clip
parcheesi	el parchís
pardon me	perdón, dispense
park	el parque
parking space	el aparcamiento
passenger	un pasajero
passport	el pasaporte
path	el camino
patient	paciente
patio	el patio
peach	un melocotón
peanuts	los cacahuetes
pear	una pera
peas	los guisantes
pen	una pluma
pencil	un lápiz

English	Spanish	English	Spanish
pentagon	un pentágono	quilting	hacer adredones
pepper	la pimienta	rabbit	el conejo, la coneja
Persian	el persa	radish	el rábano
pharmacy	la farmacia	raincoat	un impermeable
photography	la fotografía	rap	el rap
piano	el piano	rare	poco cocido
pie	la tarta, el pastel	raspberry	una frambuesa
pilot	un/una piloto	rat	una rata
pinball	la máquina del millón	reading	la lectura
ping pong	el tenis de mesa, ping-pong	receptionist	un/una recepcionista
pink	rosado	rectangle	un rectángulo
pistachios	los pistachos	red	rojo
plane	el avión	red hair	el cabello o pelo rojo
plane ticket	un billete de avión	refrigerator	un refrigerador, una nevera
plate	un plato	restaurant	el restaurante
playful	guasón	rice	el arroz
please	por favor	rice pudding	el arroz con leche
plum	una ciruela	right	a la derecha
plumber	un plomero, una plomera	ring	un anillo
poker	el póquer	road	la calle
Poland	Polonia	roast beef	el rosbif
police officer	un/una policía	rock and roll	el rock and roll
police station	la comisaría	romance movie	una película romántica
Polish	el polaco	romantic comedy	una comedia romántica
pool (for swimming)	la piscina	room	el cuarto, la pieza
pool (game)	el billar americano	round trip ticket	un billete de ida y vuelta
porch	la veranda	rubber band	una goma
pork	el cerdo	rubber stamps	las estampillas de goma
Portuguese	el portugués	rug	un tapete
post office	la oficina de correos	rugby	el rugby
poster	un cartel, un póster	ruler	una regla
pot	una cazuela, una olla	rummy	el rummy
potato	la patata, la papa	running	correr
pottery	la alfarería	Russia	Rusia
pretty please	porfis, por favorcito	Russian	el ruso
printer	una impresora	RV	la caravana pequeña
Professor	profesor	sad	triste
Puerto Rican	puertorriqueño	sailboat	el barco de vela
purple	violeta	sailing	la navegación a vela
purse	una bolsa	salad	la ensalada
pyramid	una pirámide	salt	la sal

English	Spanish	English	Spanish
same here	igualmente	sink (in kitchen)	un fregadero
sandals	unas sandalias	sink (in bathroom)	un lavabo
sandbox	el cajón de arena	sister	la hermana
sandwich	el bocadillo, el sándwich	sitcom	una comedia de situación
Saturday	sábado	six	seis
saucer	un platillo	sixteen	dieciséis
sausage	la salchicha	sixty	sesenta
saxophone	el saxofón	skateboard	el monopatín
scarf	una bufanda	skateboarding	el monopatinaje
school	una escuela	skates	los patines
science	la ciencia	skating	el patinaje
scissors	las tijeras	skiing	esquiar
scooter	el scooter, el ciclomotor	skirt	una falda
scrapbook	el álbum de recortes	slide	el tobogán
screen door	una puerta con mosquitera	slippers	unas zapatillas
sculpture	la escultura	small	pequeño
seafood	el marisco	smart	inteligente
search engine	un motor de búsqueda	smoothie	el licuado (de frutas)
secretary	un secretario, una secretaria	snake	una serpiente
security check	el control de seguridad	sneakers	unos deportivos
See you later	Hasta luego, Hasta pronto, Hasta la vista	snobbish	esnob
		soap opera	una telenovela
See you next week	Hasta la semana próxima	soccer	el fútbol
See you tomorrow	Hasta mañana	social studies	los estudios sociales
September	septiembre	socks	unos calcetines
serious	serio	soda/pop	el refresco
seven	siete	software	el software
seventeen	diecisiete	solitaire	el solitario
seventy	setenta	son	el hijo
sewing	la costura	soup	la sopa
shirt	una camisa	south	sur
shoes	unos zapatos	spades	las picas
short	bajo	Spain	España
short hair	el cabello o pelo corto	Spaniard	el español, la española
shorts	unos pantalones cortos	Spanish	el español
shoulder	el hombro	spatula	una espátula
shower	una ducha	spell checker	el corrector ortográfico
shuttle	un servicio de autobús	spelling	la ortografía
shy	tímido	sphere	una esfera
sick	enfermo	spinach	las espinacas
sidewalk	la acera	spoon	una cuchara

English	Spanish	English	Spanish
sports jacket	una chaqueta sport	teacher	un profesor, una profesora
spring	la primavera	teenager	un/una joven
square	un cuadrado	telephone	un teléfono
stairway	la escalera	television	una televisión
staple	una grapa	ten	diez
stapler	una grapadora	tennis	el tenis
star	una estrella	terminal	la terminal
stationery store	la papelería	test	un examen
steak	el bistec	thank you	gracias
stereo	un estéreo	Thank you so much!	¡Cuánto se (te) lo agradezco!
stomach	el estómago	thank you very much	muchas gracias
stove	una estufa, una cocina	theater	el teatro
straight ahead	todo seguido	thin	delgado
straight hair	el cabello o pelo liso	thirsty	sed
strawberry	una fresa	thirteen	trece
strong	fuerte	thirty	treinta
student	un/una estudiante	This is...	Este es...
student desk	un pupitre	three	tres
studious	estudioso	thumb	el pulgar
study	el despacho	Thursday	jueves
stupid	estúpido	tie	una corbata
subway	el metro	tights	unas pantimedias
sugar	el azúcar	tiny	pequeñito
suit	un traje	tip	la propina
summer	el verano	tip included	servicio incluido
Sunday	domingo	tired	cansado
sunglasses	unas gafas de sol	to be hungry	tener hambre
supermarket	el supermercado	to be thirsty	tener sed
sweater	un suéter	to board	embarcar
swimming	la natación	to brush (hair, teeth)	cepillarse
swing	el columpio	to buy a ticket	comprar un billete
Swiss	suizo	to comb (hair)	peinarse
Switzerland	Suiza	to cook	cocinar
table	una mesa	to do laundry	lavar la ropa
tall	alto	to do the dishes	lavar los platos
tanned	bronceado	to do the shopping	hacer las compras
tap dance	el claqué	to drink	beber
tape	la cinta adhesiva	to eat	comer
tarantula	una tarántula	to fall asleep	dormirse
taxi	el taxi	to get dressed	vestirse
tea	el té	to get ready	arreglarse

English	Spanish
to get tired	cansarse
to get up	levantarse
to go to bed	acostarse
to land	aterrizar
to make a reservation	hacer una reservación
to make the bed	hacer la cama
to mop the floor	fregar el suelo
to mow the lawn	cortar el césped
to print	imprimir
to put on clothes	ponerse
to put on makeup	maquillarse, pintarse
to put the house in order	arreglar la casa
to read	leer
to save	archivar
to shave	afeitarse
to straighten up	poner en orden
to sweep the floor	barrer el suelo
to take a bath	bañarse
to take a shower	ducharse
to take off	despegar
to take off clothes	quitarse
to take out the garbage	sacar la basura
to type	escribir a máquina
to vacuum	pasar la aspiradora
to wake up	despertarse
to wash (up)	lavarse
to write	escribir
to write in cursive	escribir en cursiva
toast	el pan tostado
toe	el dedo del pie
tomato	el tomate
tooth	el diente
tornado	un tornado
trail	la pista
train	el tren
tree	el árbol
triangle	un triángulo
tricycle	el triciclo
truck	el camión
trumpet	la trompeta

English	Spanish
T-shirt	una camiseta
Tuesday	martes
turkey	el pavo
turtle	una tortuga marina
TV show	un programa de televisión
TV station	una cadena de televisión
twelve	doce
twenty	veinte
two	dos
typewriter	una máquina de escribir
ugly	feo
uncle	el tío
undershirt	una camiseta
underwear	unos calzoncillos
United States	Estados Unidos
up	arriba
Valentine's Day	el Día de San Valentín
van	la camioneta
vanilla	la vainilla
veal	la ternera
video game	un videojuego
Vietnamese	el vietnamita
violin	el violín
visa	un visado
volleyball	el vóleibol
waiter, waitress	un camarero, una camerera
walking	a pie
wall	una pared
wallet	una cartera
walnuts	las nueces
washer	una lavadora
watch	un reloj
water	el agua
wavy hair	el cabello o pelo ondulado
weak	débil
weaving	el tejido
Web page	una página web
Web site	un sitio web
Wednesday	miércoles
well done	muy cocido
west	oeste

English	Spanish
what	qué
What does ____ mean?	¿Qué quiere decir ____?
What's new?	¿Qué hay de nuevo?
What's your name?	¿Cómo te llamas?
when	cuándo
where	dónde
Where are you from?	¿De dónde eres?
Where are you going?	¿Adónde vas?
Where do you live?	¿Dónde vives?
Where is the...?	¿Dónde está...?
whisk	un batidor
white	blanco
who	quién
Who are you?	¿Quién eres?
why	por qué
wide	ancho
wife	la esposa
window	una ventana
wine	el vino
winter	el invierno
woman	una mujer
wooden spoon	una cuchara de madera
woodworking	la carpintería
word processor	un procesador de textos
wrestling	la lucha
wrist	la muñeca
writer	un escritor, una escritora
writing	la escritura
yard	el jardín
yellow	amarillo
yes	sí
yogurt	el yogur
young	joven
you're welcome	de nada
zero	cero

Fun Books and Web Sites

The *Everything KIDS' Learning Spanish Book* helps you to start learning Spanish, but there are a lot of other great books and Web sites that can help you learn and practice even more.

Books

The Everything KIDS' First Spanish Puzzle and Activity Book, by Laura K. Lawless and Beth L. Blair
A whole book of Spanish puzzles and activities to help you have fun while you practice your Spanish.

Berlitz Kid's Spanish Picture Dictionary, by Berlitz International
See a picture of every word you look up.

Beth Manners' Fun Spanish for Kids
A book and CD with Spanish stories, songs, and vocabulary for kids.

Las puertas retorcidas, The Scariest Way in the World to Learn Spanish! by Dr. Kathie Dior
Learn Spanish while reading and listening to a scary story about a house with twisted doors!
www.home.thetwisteddoors.com

Learn Spanish Together, by Marie-Clair Antoine
Activities, songs, and stickers make it fun to study Spanish.

Web sites

Spanish for Children
Learn the alphabet, colors, and more with this interactive Web site.
www.angelfire.com/de/cuento/color/inicial0.html

StoryPlace
An online library for kids, with all kinds of stories and activities.
www.storyplace.org/sp/storyplace.asp

Viva Spanish
Lessons and practice on all kinds of useful Spanish vocabulary.
www.vivaspanish.org

page 3 • Alphabet Code

What kind of insect
does well in school?

AH
A

ESeh PEH EH ELeh ELeh EE ENeh HEH
S P E L L I N G

BEH EH EH
B E E

page 6 • Jumping Numbers

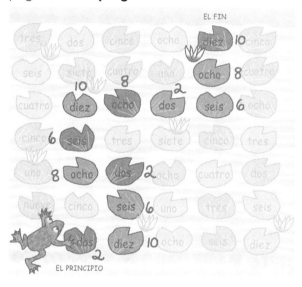

page 12 • Hey You!

page 19 • Night and Day

page 22 • Hi, Llama!

page 24 • Questions, Questions

Puzzle Answers

page 39 • Face to Face

"Yo" means "I."

I see <u>with</u> my <u>eyes</u>.
Yo veo <u>con</u> mis <u>ojos</u>.

I smell <u>with</u> my <u>nose</u>.
Yo huelo <u>con</u> mi <u>nariz</u>.

I hear <u>with</u> my <u>ears</u>.
Yo oigo <u>con</u> mis <u>orejas</u>.

I eat <u>with</u> my <u>mouth</u>.
Yo como <u>con</u> mi <u>boca</u>.

I taste <u>with</u> my <u>tongue</u>.
Yo pruebo <u>con</u> mi <u>lengua</u>.

page 49 • Gotta Go!

UNO	DÓNDE	EL HIJO
ESTÁ	PAPÁ	OCHO
ROJO	EL	AZUL
LA TÍA	SEIS	BAÑO
POR	VERDE	FAVOR

¿DÓNDÉ ESTÁ EL BAÑO, POR FAVOR?

page 58 • My Room

UNA CAMA (a bed)

page 69 • Reading List

What do all students need to read?

| U | letter right after T |
| N | letter just before O |

L	letter between K and M
I	the ninth letter
B	the second letter
R	the second letter after P
O	letter right after N

page 44 • All Around Town

1. The library
2. The school
3. The park
4. The post office
5. The supermarket

page 72 • Dressed for Work

EL CASCO
EL ABRIGO
LOS GUANTES
LOS PANTALONES
LAS BOTAS

EL PERRO

page 84 • **Nice Party**

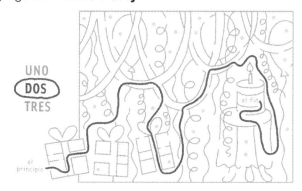

page 92 • **Let's Eat Lunch!**

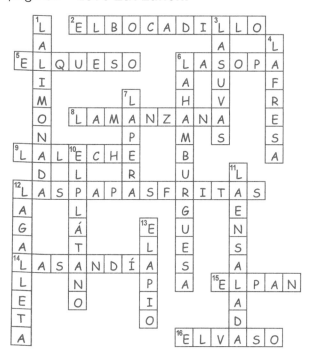

page 97 • **Hidden Foods**

1. Food fight! Sp**lat art**! A**nnoy mom**!

2. In a tun**nel, a car** never goes fast.

3. A mo**rsel, Pa**. Not a lot!

4. I eat foo**d of land** and sea.

5. I will fi**ll a salad** bowl.

page 105 • **Tricky Traveler**

I		J	U	S	T		F	L	E	W		I	N	
F	R	O	M		E	S	P	A	Ñ	A	.			
¡	M	I	S		B	R	A	Z	O	S		S	O	N
M	U	Y		C	A	N	S	A	D	O	S	!		

page 111 • **I Win!**

♣ =A
♥ =D
♦ =L
♛ =M
♠ =S

What familiar game is played with a lot of jumping?

♦♣♠ ♥♣♛♣♠

L A S   D A M A S

KEY: 20 ~~JUMP ROPE~~ 21 ~~HOPSCOTCH~~ 22 CHECKERS

page 117 • **Nifty Knitter**

WORD LIST
3 el corazón *heart*
1 el pollo *chicken*
6 el gusano *worm*
2 el diamante *diamond*
4 la llave *key*
5 la cometa *kite*

The Everything® Kids' Series

The Everything® Kids' Animal Puzzle & Activity Book
1-59337-305-8

The Everything® Kids' Baseball Book, 4th Ed.
1-59337-614-6

The Everything® Kids' Bible Trivia Book
1-59337-031-8

The Everything® Kids' Bugs Book
1-58062-892-3

The Everything® Kids' Cars and Trucks
Puzzle and Activity Book
1-59337-703-7

The Everything® Kids' Christmas Puzzle & Activity Book
1-58062-965-2

The Everything® Kids' Cookbook
1-58062-658-0

The Everything® Kids' Crazy Puzzles Book
1-59337-361-9

The Everything® Kids' Dinosaurs Book
1-59337-360-0

The Everything® Kids' First Spanish
Puzzle and Activity Book
1-59337-717-7

The Everything® Kids' Gross Hidden Pictures Book
1-59337-615-4

The Everything® Kids' Gross Jokes Book
1-59337-448-8

The Everything® Kids' Gross Mazes Book
1-59337-616-2

The Everything® Kids' Gross Puzzle & Activity Book
1-59337-447-X

The Everything® Kids' Halloween Puzzle &
Activity Book
1-58062-959-8

The Everything® Kids' Hidden Pictures Book
1-59337-128-4

The Everything® Kids' Horses Book
1-59337-608-1

The Everything® Kids' Joke Book
1-58062-686-6

The Everything® Kids' Knock Knock Book
1-59337-127-6

The Everything® Kids' Learning Spanish Book
1-59337-716-9

The Everything® Kids' Math Puzzles Book
1-58062-773-0

The Everything® Kids' Mazes Book
1-58062-558-4

The Everything® Kids' Money Book
1-58062-685-8

The Everything® Kids' Nature Book
1-58062-684-X

The Everything® Kids' Pirates Puzzle and Activity Book
1-59337-607-3

The Everything® Kids' Princess Puzzle and Activity Book
1-59337-704-5

The Everything® Kids' Puzzle Book
1-58062-687-4

The Everything® Kids' Riddles & Brain Teasers Book
1-59337-036-9

The Everything® Kids' Science Experiments Book
1-58062-557-6

The Everything® Kids' Sharks Book
1-59337-304-X

The Everything® Kids' Soccer Book
1-58062-642-4

The Everything® Kids' Travel Activity Book
1-58062-641-6

All titles are $6.95 or $7.95 unless otherwise noted.

Available wherever books are sold!
To order, call 800-258-0929, or visit us at *www.adamsmedia.com*
Everything® and everything.com® are registered trademarks of F+W Publications, Inc.
Prices subject to change without notice.